Coaching Authentic Retirement

Coaching Authentic Retirement™

Helping Retirees and Pre-retirees Plan their Retirement Lifestyle

Marcia Bench

Coaching Authentic Retirement™
Published by Coaching and Training Solutions, LLC dba High Flight Press 2004

Copyright © 2004 by Marcia Bench
All rights reserved.

Reproduction or translation of any part of work beyond that permitted by the 1976 United States Copyright Act without the express written permission of the copyright owner is unlawful. Requests for permission or further information should be addressed to Permissions Department, High Flight Press, P.O. Box 5778, Lake Havasu City, AZ 86404.

This publication is designed to provide accurate and authoritative information in regard to the subject matter covered. It is sold with the understanding that the publisher is not engaged in rendering professional services. If legal, accounting, medical, psychological, or any other expert assistance is required, the services of a competent professional person should be sought. Author and publisher specifically disclaim any liability for the reader's use of any forms or advice provided in this book. It is not warranted as fit for any specific use or purpose, but is intended to give general information that is as current as possible as of the date of publication.

Library of Congress Cataloging-in-Publication Data:

Bench, Marcia
    Coaching Authentic Retirement
    / Marcia Bench
    ISBN 0-9759655-5-7
    1. Coaching 2. Retirement 3. Lifestyle 4. Psychology

Printed in the United States of America

TABLE OF CONTENTS

INTRODUCTION & COURSE OVERVIEW 9
1. The Retirement Wave: Facts and Figures 11
   Learning Objectives: 11
   The Retirement Wave 11
   Contributing Trends 12
   Wealth and Financial Status of the 50-Somethings 13
   Are People Retiring Earlier or Later? 14
   Longevity and Health Care 14
   Family Responsibilities 15
   "Retirees" and Work 15
   The Retirement Coach's Role 16
   Case Study: 17
2. Redefining Retirement; Timing; & the Authentic Retirement™ Model 19
   Learning Objectives: 19
   Review of Chapter 1: 19
   Redefining Retirement 19
   Timing One's Retirement 21
   The Authentic Retirement™ Model 25
   Case Studies 29
3. Financial and Lifestyle Issues 31
   Learning Objectives: 31
   Review of Chapter 2: 31
   Financial Issues in Retirement Planning 31
   Beliefs About Money 34
   To Relocate or Not to Relocate? 38
   Finding Your Retirement Destination 39
   You're Never Too Young to Learn 41
4. Emotional Adjustments 43
   Learning Objectives: 43
   Review of Chapter 3: 43
   The Nature of Transition 43
   Models of the Process 44
   "Coper" and "Thriver" Approaches to Facing Transition 47
   Applying the Coper/Thriver Approaches 52
   Overcoming Fear 52
   Dangers of Boredom 53
   Case Study: 54
5. Work Issues 57
   Learning Objectives: 57
   Review of Chapter 4: 57
   To Work or Not to Work, that is the Question 57
   Work Options for Retired/Retiring Clients 59
      Keeping Current Job 59
      Working part-time at prior job 60

- Changing Careers 60
- Taking a Sabbatical 61
- Becoming an Entrepreneur – Traditional or Social 61
- Mentoring 62
- Contract or temporary work 63
- Pursue a work substitute (e.g. volunteering) 63
- Age Discrimination and Retirement 64
- The Importance of a Self-Employed Mindset 66
- Generational Issues at Work 68
- Case Study: 69

6. Reinventing Identity 73
- Learning Objectives: 73
- Review of Chapter 5: 73
- Existential Questions Emerge Again 73
- Allowing Authenticity 75
- Life Purpose Revisited 77
  - Definitions of Life Purpose 77
  - Qualities of Life Purpose 78
  - Why It's Important 78
  - Clues to Life Purpose 79
  - Obstacles to Discovering Life Purpose 81
  - Examples of Purpose Statements 82
  - Implementing Life Purpose 83
- Living in the Moment 86

7. Health and Aging 87
- Learning Objectives: 87
- Review of Chapter 5: 87
- New Vistas of Health 87
- Longer Life: Challenge or Opportunity? 89
- Myths and Fears About Aging 91
- Health Care and Insurance 92
- When Health Issues Arise 93
- Case Study 95

8. Social/Relationship Shifts 97
- Learning Objectives: 97
- Review of Chapter 7: 97
- Impact of Retirement on Couples 97
- Top Five Areas That Affect A Couple's Relationship Retirement Transition When One or Both Retire 99
  - 1. Managing Income and Taxes 99
  - 2. Maintaining Communication 99
  - 3. Compromising 101
  - 4. Role Assignments 102
  - 5. Gratification 103
- Reactions of Family and Friends 103
- Weaving the Social Web 104

- Sandwich Generation 105
- Grandparent or Parent? 106
- Case Study 107

9. Leisure and Travel; Retirement Assessments 109
- Learning Objectives: 109
- Review of Chapter 8: 109
- Leisure in Retirement 109
- Travel: Adventure or Escape? 110
  - RV'ing 112
- Retirement Assessments 113
  1. Retirement Options. 113
  2. Retirement Satisfaction Inventory. 114
  3. Dr. Nancy Schlossberg. 114
  4. Sedlar/Miners Quiz. 114
  5. Retirement Stress Inventory. 115
  6. Application of Other Assessments to Retirement. 115

10. Varieties of Retirement Lifestyles 117
- Learning Objectives: 117
- Review of Chapter 9: 117
- Elements of a Retirement Life 117
- Examples 118

11. The Retiring Workforce: Another Side of the Retirement Wave 123
- Learning Objectives: 123
- Review of Chapter 10: 123
- Issues for Employers of Retiring Boomers 123
- Lack of Employer Awareness 123
- Roots of Early Retirement 125
- Employer versus Retiree Needs: a Disconnect 125
- The Discrimination Issue 127
- The Costs of Hiring 127
- Appealing to Gen X 127
- The Employer Response 128

12. Filling Your Retirement Coaching Practice 131
- Learning Objectives: 131
- Review of Chapter 11: 131
- A 10-Step Plan for Marketing Retirement Coaching 131
  1. Define what kind of retirement coach you want to be. 131
  - Figure 17: THE GEMS™ APPROACH TO MARKETING 132
  2. Determine what products and services you will offer. 133
  3. Develop vision for your ideal practice. 133
  4. Use the Internet to build awareness. 133
  5. Start an ezine – and write articles for others. 134
  6. Give teleclasses and speak at service and professional groups. 135
  7. Cultivate referrals through strategic alliances. 136
  8. Develop relationships with and coverage by local and national media. 136
  9. Track your efforts and results; set and re-set priorities. 136

    10. Expand your practice. 137
    CONTENTS OF RETIREMENT COACHES TOOLBOX 139
RETIREMENT COACHES TOOLBOX.. 141
  1. Retirement Readiness Wheel.. 141
  2. Ideal Retirement Exercise 142
  3. Authentic Retirement Worksheet No. 1 143
  4. Authentic Retirement Worksheet No. 2 147
  5. Authentic Retirement Worksheet No. 3 150
    My Motivators 150
    Interests.. 151
  6. Authentic Retirement Worksheet No. 4 153
  7. Authentic Retirement Worksheet No. 5 155
  8. Authentic Retirement Worksheet No. 6 158
  9. Authentic Retirement Worksheet No. 7 161
    Partner Profile.. 162
  10. Authentic Retirement Worksheet No. 8 164
  11. My Beliefs About Money... 166
  12. Coper/Thriver Quiz 168
  13. Coaching Questions For Each Thriver Trait Cluster 171
  14. Should I Work In Retirement? 173
  15. Is Entrepreneurship Right For You?.. 174
  16. My Retirement Health... 175
  17. Top Ten Indicators To Refer To A Mental Health Professional 177
  18. My Social Network.. 181
  19. What Will I Do With My Time?.. 183
  20. Retirement Satisfaction Inventory... 187
  21. Retirement Lifestyle Template™ 191
  22. My Retirement Lifestyle Profile 195
  23. Marketing Priorities Checklist 196
    Category 196
  24. Resources for Retirement Coaches 199
About the Author... 203
COACHING & TRAINING SOLUTIONS PRODUCT CATALOG............................ 204

INTRODUCTION & COURSE OVERVIEW

Over 10,000 people turn 55 each day in the U.S. (1,000 in Canada). Most will retire for the first time, unsuccessfully, at age 57. Why "unsuccessfully"? Because while many pre-retirees plan and calculate their financial resources to ensure an adequate nest egg to fund their retirement, almost none of them invest time and energy planning the *nonfinancial* aspects of retiring. For example:

- How will I spend my time when I'm no longer working full-time?
- Do I expect retirement to consist of full-time leisure? How do I know that will be satisfying for me? And if not, what *does* retirement mean for me?
- Do I want to continue working in a business or position of my choice? How many hours? Who would employ me, or what business would I start?
- What is my attitude toward the transition to retirement? Do I know how to address my fears?
- How will my marriage and other family and social relationships change when I retire? Do I have a vision of how I would like those new relationships to be?
- Who am I apart from my job?
- What is my current level of health? Do I know how to maintain it? Do I have a plan if it changes?
- How do I interact successfully with co-workers from generations other than mine?
- What is my vision for an ideal retirement?
- What primary contribution do I want to make in the "third half" of my life?
- What motivates me?

These questions and many more are rarely asked by people approaching retirement. As a result, they end up dissatisfied, or consider returning to work, or wish they'd planned it better. Retirement coaches can help their clients avoid these undesirable scenarios!

We predict that the retiring Baby Boomers will have such a substantial impact on reinventing retirement that it will be amazing! But at this juncture, we are literally "writing the rules as we go." What will retirement mean going forward? Will we even use that word any more? This book and course are designed to answer those questions.

This book is the text used to train retirement coaches through the program offered by Retirement Coach Institute http://www.retirementcoachinstitute.com. If you have found it elsewhere, we invite you to visit our web site and consider becoming a

Certified Professional Retirement Coach™. And if you are enrolled in our Coaching Authentic Retirement™ class, welcome! We invite you to read each of the chapters prior to listening to the class session held to discuss that topic, and to email your questions, comments, and experiences to us at coach@retirementcoachinstitute.com Certification requirements are outlined on the RCI web site at http://www.retirementcoachinstitute.com, so please consult the Internet for details.

Happy learning!

Marcia Bench

1. THE RETIREMENT WAVE: FACTS AND FIGURES

"Don't think of retiring from the world until the world will be sorry that you retire."
                                                         Samuel Johnson

Learning Objectives:

1. Realize the magnitude of the retirement wave of which your clients are a part
2. Explore the many areas of life and society that are – and will be – affected by the retirement wave

The Retirement Wave

As between 70 and 80 million "Baby Boomers" – born between 1946 and 1964 – approach retirement, it is clear that something significant is happening! Perhaps one of the first to see this wave coming was Dr. Ken Dychtwald, author of *Age Wave* and related books. He points out other ways in which Boomers have transformed society:

- Boomers didn't just eat food – they transformed the snack, restaurant, and supermarket industries
- Boomers didn't just buy cars – they transformed the auto industry
- They didn't just go to work – they transformed the workplace

And so on, throughout the life cycle. From birth to retirement, whole institutions and industries have transformed and evolved to meet the needs (and wants!) of this huge generation. To get an idea of how large this cohort (or group within the population) really is, consider these facts:

- In the U.S., 10,000 people turn 55 everyday, or one every 7.5 seconds; in Canada, over 1,000 people per day do so (*The New Retirement* by Richard Johnson Ph.D.)
- Over 50's currently constitute 27 percent of the total population and 36 percent of all adults (Ken Dychtwald)
- The number of people 65 and over will increase from the current 40 million (14 percent of total) to 70 million (20 percent of total) [i.e., nearly double in size] between 2010 and 2030 (*Don't Retire, Rewire!* By Jeri Sedlar and Rick Miners)

A recent United Nations survey looked at the projected growth in percentage of the population age 65 and older, 2000 to 2020, among various countries. See Figure 1 for a comparison.

Figure 1: Growth in Population 65 and Above

Country	2000	2020	% Change (2000- 2020)
Japan	17.1	28.2	53.7
Canada	12.8	18.2	42.9
Australia	12.1	16.8	39.2
New Zealand	11.6	15.6	33.7
USA	12.5	16.6	32.8
Germany	16.4	21.8	31.9
France	15.9	20.1	26.4
UK	16.0	19.8	23.6

NOTES:

Contributing Trends

The growth in sheer numbers of over-65 people in the population is significant in itself. But several other trends make the retirement wave of Boomers even more remarkable:

- America is facing an impending crisis of skilled workers as soon as 2010, by which it could encounter a deficit of over 10 million skilled workers needed to fill jobs vacated by the Boomers and incapable of being filled by the smaller generation that follows (*Impending Crisis,* Roger Herman et al; *Age Works,* Beverly Goldberg). More on this in chapter 11.

- Many who planned to retire early can no longer do so due to the downturn in the stock market in the late 20th century. Over 70 percent of pre-retirees recently surveyed by AARP (the American Association of Retired Persons) plan to work at least part-time during retirement.

- Due to the so-called "downaging" phenomenon – as well as advances in medicine and health care – older people are far healthier than their peers just a decade earlier; 60-year-olds are as healthy as 40- or 50-year-olds were 10 years ago. The increasing life expectancy extends retirement and means that retirement is no longer a time of decline, but of new beginnings. The individual must now design his/her own retirement lifestyle! We address this in chapter 7.

Have these trends begun to affect you? How?

What are the implications of these trends for retirement coaches?

Wealth and Financial Status of the 50-Somethings

- The stock market swallowed about 530 billion dollars in U.S. retirement savings (Federal Reserve Board data quoted in Ellen Hoffman's "The New Retirement," *Readers Digest* July 2003)
- People over 50 earn over 2 trillion dollars in annual income and own more than 70 percent of the financial assets in America; they control more than 7 trillion dollars in wealth (Ken Dychtwald)
- Over-50's represent a full half of the discretionary spending power (Ken Dychtwald)
- Baby Boomers (totaling 76 million people) will reach their peak spending at ages 45 to 50, which will be from 2004 to 2009 (*Impending Crisis,* Roger Herman et al)
- Many are not making adequate financial preparations for retirement (per Economic Policy Institute, quoted in *Impending Crisis):*
    - 37 percent of those saving for retirement say they are doing only a fair job of managing their retirement portfolios, and 7 percent say they are doing a poor job
    - 44 percent of those saving for retirement say they expect to live *less* comfortably in retirement
    - 29 percent of retirees say their standard of living has gone down in retirement

Do these trends make retiring Boomers more or less suited to/appropriate for coaching?

Are People Retiring Earlier or Later?

- People are retiring earlier; the average first retirement is at age 57 (*The New Retirement* by Richard Johnson Ph.D.)
- But on the other hand, one out of eight people over age 65 was in the workforce in 2000 (Mary Williams Walsh, "Reversing Decades-Long Trend, Americans Retiring Later in Life," *New York Times,* 2/26/01)
- Nearly two-thirds of people retire at age 62 (*Age Works,* Beverly Goldberg) – and many before that!
- A June 2003 study done by AARP indicated that 21 percent of people who had not yet retired (among the Baby Boomer cohort) have now postponed retirement until at least age 70, due in part to stock market losses during the past three years (for details see full study at http://research.aarp.org/econ/multiwork_2003_1.pdf -- a recommended read!)
- Forty-five percent of the US government employees will be eligible for retirement in 2005 (US Dept. of Labor statistics)

What have you noticed among retirees you know – or those who are eligible to retire in the next few years – regarding earlier vs. later timing for their retirement?

Longevity and Health Care

Consider these facts:

- The average Baby Boomer can expect to live to the age of 83 (Hudson Institute and government sources)
- In the past 90 years, longevity in western culture has increased 30 years (*The New Retirement,* by Dr. Richard Johnson)
- The US Census Bureau estimates that there could be anywhere from 250,000 to 4 million centenarians living in the US by 2050 (Hudson Institute)
- Over-50's consume over 74 percent of all prescription drugs and represent 65 percent of all hospital bed-stays (Ken Dychtwald)

What effects does longer life expectancy have on retiree and pre-retiree clients' retirement planning?

Family Responsibilities

The Retirement Wave is changing families too:

- According to 2000 census data, 4.5 million children are living with their grandparents, up 30 percent since 1990; the number of grandparents responsible for these grandchildren's needs is at least 2.4 million (AARP)
- These same grandparents may be caring for an ailing spouse and have their own health care concerns

How does this lifestyle factor impact coaching of retirees?

"Retirees" and Work

And needless to say, work will never be the same as Boomers retire and seek new options:

- Almost half of the nearly 70 percent of workers who have not yet retired envision working into their 70's or beyond (AARP)
- The top five reasons for working in retirement, according to the AARP survey, are:
    1. Desire to stay mentally active (83%)
    2. Desire to stay physically active (80%)
    3. Desire to remain productive or useful (76%)
    4. Desire to do something fun or enjoyable (66%)
    5. You'll need the health benefits (56%), tied with Desire to help other people (also 56%)
- Top five types of work planned or being done in retirement, as found by the AARP survey:
    1. Professional specialties (20%)
    2. Skilled/semi-skilled labor (14%)
    3. Service and protective workers (13%)
    4. Sales (11%)
    5. White color/clerical (non supervisory) (7%)

- The international perspective: As life expectancy increases, so too is the anticipated participation rate in the workforce for people age 60 and older. See Figure 2 below.

Figure 2 - OECD Survey of Work Participation

Country	1970	1995	2030
Japan	9.3	12.5	20.7
USA	9.1	5.8	9.8
UK	9.0	5.3	8.1
Canada	6.9	4.2	8.1
Australia	6.4	3.6	6.3
New Zealand	6.5	3.3	5.3
Germany	9.3	2.9	5.5
France	7.9	2.5	4.0

- The average time spent at a job is projected to continue plummeting: in 1990 it was 4.6 years, by 2000 3.5 years;
- However, the length of the job search for older job seekers has been found to be twice as long as that of people under 30 ("Career Choices and Challenges of Younger and Older Workers," Drake Beam Morin 11/06/01)

Can you think of other aspects of life and society that are or will be affected by the Retirement Wave?

The Retirement Coach's Role

Given all of these trends, the retirement coach can become overwhelmed and perhaps confused in determining his/her appropriate role. Retirement coaching can be defined as follows:

> "Retirement coaching is an interactive process of exploring all aspects of the retirement lifestyle and plans toward it – leading to effective action – in which the coach acts as both a *catalyst* and *facilitator* of the individual's discovery process to determine a lifestyle that matches the individual's values, priorities and purpose as well as applicable organizational goals."
> -- Marcia Bench, MCCC

Following is a summary of appropriate and inappropriate roles for us as retirement coaches:

- Retirement coaches do:
  - Help clients set priorities, develop a plan and timeline, work toward it
  - Assist clients determine whether they will work, and how it will be structured if they do
  - Help clients overcome fears and other mental and emotional barriers
  - Test clients' assumptions, ideas and models about retirement
  - Assist clients in resolving timing issues (spouse works, they don't), factor in needs for care of family members, etc.
  - Brainstorm with clients ideas for entrepreneurship in retirement
  - Help companies address retention issues, avoid talent loss through flexwork and similar programs

- Retirement coaches do not:
  - Advise clients on investments or financial portfolio
  - Provide health care (including mental health)
  - Sell insurance or other needed coverages or benefits
  - Provide legal services in drafting living trust, will, power of attorney, health care directive, and the like

But note: the professionals that *do* provide these services are great partners for the retirement coach!

Case Study:

You have been approached by a prospective new client named Phillip, age 55. He is married, has two grown children, and two grandchildren. He currently works as Chief Technology Officer at Technology Plus, a software firm that manufactures and distributes software for children. Though he has been with Technology Plus since its inception in 1998– including a successful IPO (initial public offering) in 2000 – he changed jobs frequently prior to that. He has retirement savings of about $250,000 and his annual salary is currently $120,000.

He is thinking about retirement, and had in fact planned to retire at age 58 – but now feels he may need to defer retiring because (a) his divorced daughter has progressive multiple sclerosis and is losing the ability to care for her children – so he and his wife may need to take them in, and (b) he lost about half of his retirement portfolio in the recent stock market downturn.

1. What would you want Phillip to know about the Retirement Wave as it pertains to him?

2. What questions would you want to ask him to determine whether coaching would benefit him?

3. What do you see as the key issues for Phillip as he approaches retirement?

NOTES:

KEY CONCEPTS LEARNED:

Coaching Authentic Retirement 19

2. REDEFINING RETIREMENT; TIMING; & THE AUTHENTIC RETIREMENT™ MODEL

"Retire when the work is done. This is the way of heaven."
— *Tao Te Ching*

Learning Objectives:

1. Explore new meanings and terms for "retirement"
2. Learn to help clients time their retirement
3. Discover the 8 key elements of the Authentic Retirement™ Model
4. Learn how to use the Authentic Retirement with clients

Review of Chapter 1:

Each week we begin with a review of the prior week's material. Please be prepared to discuss the following questions:

1. What birth years constitute the Baby Boomers that now form the Retirement Wave?

2. Is the number of people over 65 in the U.S. (a) growing significantly, (b) growing slightly, (c) staying stagnant or (d) declining?

3. What four trends are contributing to the retirement of the Boomers and setting the stage to transform retirement as we have known it?

Redefining Retirement

The concept of retirement did not exist until the 1930's, when then U.S. President Roosevelt established the Social Security and with it, retirement. But what does the term actually mean? According to Webster's Dictionary, to *retire* is:

> "1. to withdraw, as for rest or seclusion; 2. To go to bed; 3. To give up working or serving, usually because of advancing age; 4. To remove from active service..."

For many pre-retirees, this is *not* the meaning they want to attach to the remaining years of their lives! When life expectancy was shorter and one worked at one company until being given a pension and gold watch at 65, there wasn't typically much life left for retirement. Then, a declining model, where one's remaining life waned after work was finished, made more sense.

Interestingly, the Spanish word for retirement and pension is *jubilacion,* indicating glee. Now, when retirees may have as many as 30 to 50 years after traditional full-time work to be "retired," new terminology is needed. They are planning a whole other life in some senses, one for which a new model of life and work design must be created. Let's examine some ideas about how to redefine retirement.

A. David Stein, in his article "The New Meaning of Retirement" (ERIC Digest 217, 2000) notes that:

> *"The 21st century may be known as the era of lifelong learning and lifelong working...Retirement, the end stage of a linear working life, may be replaced with a learning, working, leisure, working, learning life cycle. In a cyclical living and working model, participating in the work force never ceases but is interspersed with periods of leisure and learning..."*

B. Author and retirement expert Ken Dychtwald, in a study of over 1000 individuals age 55 and over entitled "Revisioning Retirement," cited in the Resource List, found that the notion of retirement as a "winding down" or "extended vacation" is now obsolete. Only 22 percent of those surveyed agreed with the idea of relaxing and doing nothing as their idea of retirement.

Secondly, approximately 95 percent of pre-retirees surveyed expect to continue working in some capacity during retirement.

C. A June 2003 study done by American Association of Retired Persons ("The AARP Working in Retirement Study" – see Resource List) includes a section on Personal Definition of Retirement. It found that over 70 percent of those surveyed said "Spending more time with family and friends, receiving Social Security and pension benefits, relaxing, having more fun, and doing things you never had time for" are very much part of their retirement definition. Over half say work will also be included in their activities.

What new terms could we use for this apparently much more active, multidimensional part of life? Here are a few terms offered by our students:

- Rewirement
- Refirement
- Dynamic generation
- Ageless generation
- Age of fulfillment/Fulfillment generation
- Wind-down (part-time)

- Step-down (lower level of responsibility)
- Time-out (sabbatical)
- Ease-down (gradual reduction in hours, responsibility)
- Elder years
- Renewal years
- Re-creators
- The authentic years
- Third age
- Protirement

Can you think of others?

How do you envision your own retirement? (if you have thought about it!)

Timing One's Retirement

Even the timing of retirement is a personal decision today. And as discussed in chapter 1, many who can are choosing to retire earlier than age 65. How does one know when the time is right?

A majority of retirees surveyed in the Cornell Retirement and Well-Being Study (see Resource List) found that 64 percent of the generation just prior to the Baby Boom wished they had planned more for retirement, whether regarding health care, where to live, family changes, or leisure activities. Planning the financial side of the process was adequately done by about half of those surveyed, but the other areas lagged significantly behind.

In determining timing of the retirement decision, several areas must be examined: financial, mental, emotional, social, and personal factors (identity, health, etc.). And later in this chapter, the Retirement Wheel and the assessments discussed in chapter 9 will help clients determine whether or not they are ready to retire.

A. Financial. Another finding from the "Revisioning Retirement" study described above is that satisfaction in retirement is positively related to the number of years one saves for retirement. More than 60 percent of those who saved for 25 years or more reported being extremely satisfied with retirement. Satisfaction went down with fewer years of financial preparation.

The study identified four distinct segments of contemporary US retirement experience:

1. **Ageless Explorers,** 27 percent of the sample, personify a new ideal for retirement. Retirement can be seen as an exciting new phase in their lives as they would rather be too busy than risk being bored. These retirees have high levels of education and the highest net worth. They have saved for retirement an average of 24 years, feel prepared financially for retirement, and appear psychologically prepared to make the most out of this stage of their lives.

2. **Comfortably Contents,** 19 percent of the total, seek to live a traditional retirement lifestyle. They relax and enjoy their golden years. They aren't as interested in work or in contributing to society, and would rather be bored, are less willing to risk feeling stressed in retirement. They have saved on average 23 years and spend their time on travel and recreational activities.

3. **Live for Todays,** 22 percent, are highly interested in personal growth and reinvention and have many retirement ideals in common with group 1. Unfortunately, they appear to have been focused on living for the "here and now" and are burdened with worry that they did not adequately prepare for retirement. This group saved an average of only 18 years and they are likely to continue working in retirement.

4. **Sick and Tireds,** 32 percent, are living the worst possible scenario: less educated, and with fewer financial resources, they have low expectations for the future and may have been forced into retirement by poor health. They took few steps to prepare for retirement, and saved very little for the least number of years: 16. Of all the groups, this segment is less likely to travel, visit family, participate in community events, or tap into their human potential.

Of course, saving for retirement is one thing; feeling like the individual has saved "enough" is something else. We'll explore this issue more in chapter 3. To determine readiness, we might ask our clients:

- Do you have sufficient financial assets to support you for 30 or more years of retirement?
- If not, how will you make up the shortfall?
- How do you know you have enough?
- Are there other options you have been unwilling to consider that could allow you to retire earlier? (E.g., reduce lifestyle demands, work part-time in retirement, etc.)

- What will the tax consequences of your retirement be?

Others:

B. Mental Factors. Attitude toward retirement specifically, and aging in general, are key to the timing decision. We may want to ask our clients such questions as:

- What is your attitude toward retirement?
- Can you see opportunities for growth, not just decline, in retirement?
- Have you created a retirement vision for yourself?
- Do you know your key motivators and values that will need to be satisfied even when you are not working?
- Have you clarified your purpose in life?

What other questions might be useful regarding the client's mental state?

C. Emotional. A wide range of emotions can arise during any transition, and retirement can be one of the more significant transitions in life for many people. Alternating between elation and paralyzing fear is not uncommon as clients contemplate retirement. Chapter 4 will discuss this aspect further. We might ask such questions as:

- Are you aware of any barriers to your fully enjoying your retirement?
- [If the client keeps postponing his/her retirement date] What are you avoiding?
- How comfortable are you with less structure in your life?
- Have you taken any breaks from your professional life of two weeks or more? What was it like for you?
- Do you have hobbies or interests outside work that you enjoy?

Others:

D. Social. Developing relationships that are not work-related is another key task prior to retirement. Despite the best intentions, most people lose contact with former coworkers once they leave a job, whether to retire or to take other employment. Chapter 8 will delve into this aspect of retirement. Questions to ask clients about their social relationships might include:

- What percentage of your friends is not connected to your work or profession?
- How much time do you spend in social activities each month?
- Have you and your spouse or partner discussed the impact of retirement on your relationship?
- How do you anticipate your children will react to your retirement?

Other questions:

E. Personal. Ultimately, the decision as to when to retire is a personal one, and depends on the individual's preparation in the above aspects as well as other issues such as their identity apart from work, the role of spirituality in his/her life, overall outlook (optimistic vs. pessimistic), etc. We can query clients:

- Who are you when you don't have a job title?
- Have you answered to your satisfaction such questions as "Is there a God?" "What do I believe?" and established a life philosophy?
- Do you plan to work in retirement? If so do you have a clear focus on what you will do?
- Are you an optimist or a pessimist?
- Are you willing to change?
- Can you be flexible and adaptable to the changing circumstances and experiences of retirement?
- Are you looking forward to retirement, or dreading it?

Others:

In the book *How to Retire Happy, Wild and Free* by Ernie Zelinski, some strong signs that one is *not* ready for full-time retirement are:

- You have been unhappy all your working life and have been waiting for retirement to make you happy
- You have no nest egg because you have been expecting a big lottery win to fund your retirement dreams.
- Planning a vacation is more fun than taking it.

- Vacations have always taken a back seat to work commitments.
- You have no hobbies or other interests outside of work.
- Your best friends are people that you work with and that you don't like all that much.
- All of the social functions you attend are work related.
- The thought of spending a lot more time at home with your spouse makes you extremely anxious or dejected.
- Your spouse has always wanted you to get a life outside of work, but you haven't gotten around to it.
- You don't know the meaning of sabbatical, let alone having ever actually taken one.
- On weekends your spouse constantly complains about your getting into her or his hair.
- You persistently think of work, even when you aren't on the job.
- You are proud to be a workaholic even though you know workaholics aren't that productive.

A tool you can use to help clients assess their readiness to retire is the Retirement Readiness Wheel, Tool 1 in the Retirement Coaches Toolbox (page 141).

NOTES:

The Authentic Retirement™ Model

As we have seen, Baby Boomers don't want to "retire" as their parents and grandparents do; they want to design it anew, just as they have designed every other aspect of their lives. But how? To date, no model has been developed – and widely accepted – to help pre-retirees plan the non-financial aspects of their retirement.

Successful retirement must take into consideration all of the key elements of one's life. Financial resources are one aspect to be sure, but they are by no means the only place to focus. Authentic Retirement is a unique, comprehensive approach to retirement planning that is unlike any other system. And it is just that – a *system* or template that will help you ensure that your retirement decision is not only financially viable, but emotionally and personally satisfying as well.

Our Authentic Retirement Model includes the following eight elements:

1. **Life Purpose.** The issue of one's purpose in life arises at different times for different individuals. If clients have not confronted the meaning of their life prior to retirement, it will emerge for exploration then. And even if they have considered it previously, life without full-time work can shift their sense of identity: "Who am I if I'm not the Vice President of x?"

   Dr. Carl Jung emphasizes that to self-actualize (or fully develop as people), we must discover and embrace spirituality and a sense of purpose by our 40's or beyond. He calls this individuation. Often your retiring clients will be questioning their identity, redefining the roles of work and leisure in their lives, or desiring clarity on their life purpose. To discover it, we suggest the use of Authentic Retirement Worksheet 1, included in Retirement Coaches Toolbox (page 143), as a tool. Clients may need to reflect on their answers for days or weeks before the right phrase for the "essence" portion of their life purpose statement is clear. But by asking them questions that probe what is most meaningful and about what they have the most passion, their life purpose will emerge.

2. **Values:** A second factor one must consider in planning retirement is what values are important to the person. During clients' primary working years, those values may largely be fulfilled through work. Or raising children may fulfill family values. But how will the person ensure that their key values will also be satisfied in retirement? Planning toward that begins with increasing one's awareness about key values. Authentic Retirement Worksheet 2 in Retirement Coaches Toolbox (page 146) can be used with clients to explore their values.

3. **Motivators:** Motivators, also called "drivers," are the things that motivate a person, whether in work or in other aspects of life. For example, some people are motivated by spending their time working for a paycheck; others are highly motivated *not* to have to do so. Each client's motivators must be identified, and then incorporated into his/her retirement consciously. Lifestyle choices made with a view toward what is motivating for the client will lead to significantly greater satisfaction, in most cases, than planning merely based on what others expect the person to do, or what one's peers have chosen. Authentic Vocation Worksheet 3 (page 149) can help clients clarify this. It also inquires into the client's interests, which can shed additional light.

4. **Talents:** This factor asks, "what skills, talents, strengths and abilities do I have that I would enjoy using even if I don't get paid?" "If I want or need to work, how do I envision using them in a part-time or contract position in retirement?" In *Now Discover Your Strengths,* Marcus Buckingham and his co-author define talents as those things an individual does well naturally.

Clients may have latent talents that they have either never used or abandoned during their primary career years that can now be expressed in retirement. Authentic Retirement Worksheet 4 (page 152) can be used to clarify one's talents.

5. **Life and work experience:** Experiences from both work and other aspects of life can be leveraged in retirement. If one has extensive experience in management, for example, directing a fund-raising effort for a nonprofit organization to promote a cause about which one feels strongly can be a retirement application of that experience. Authentic Retirement Worksheet 5 (page 154) explores experience as a component of Authentic Retirement.

6. **Desired activities:** Here the client dreams, plans, and imagines the elements of his/her retirement lifestyle – or at least the first version of it! What are their dreams, plans, and other elements of your retirement lifestyle? On which activities will they focus most? Here they envision their ideal mix. See Authentic Retirement Worksheet 6 in Retirement Coaches Toolbox (page 157) for details.

7. **Lifestyle and environment** Next, the client defines how the activities from factor 6 will be blended into a retirement lifestyle. Will they live "on the road" or in the home they have owned for years? Will they spend more time with their spouse or less? Will their disposable income be higher or lower than during their working years? Or perhaps they are grandparenting as the primary caretaker for a grandchild, or dealing with a health condition. All of these factors are combined into a desired retirement lifestyle that works perfectly for clients and their unique needs. See Authentic Retirement Worksheet 7 (page 160).

8. **The Finance Factor.** Once the seven key categories of factors are clarified, the final consideration is money. Will the person's financial resources support him/her through retirement? If not, how will they make up the deficit? We leave this consideration until last to allow the creative process free reign as clients clarify what they really want in retirement; then they can creatively address the financial aspects as well. See Authentic Retirement Worksheet 8 (page 163) for questions to ask here.

Figure 3 on the next page illustrates the factors of Authentic Retirement.

Figure 3 - Authentic Retirement Model

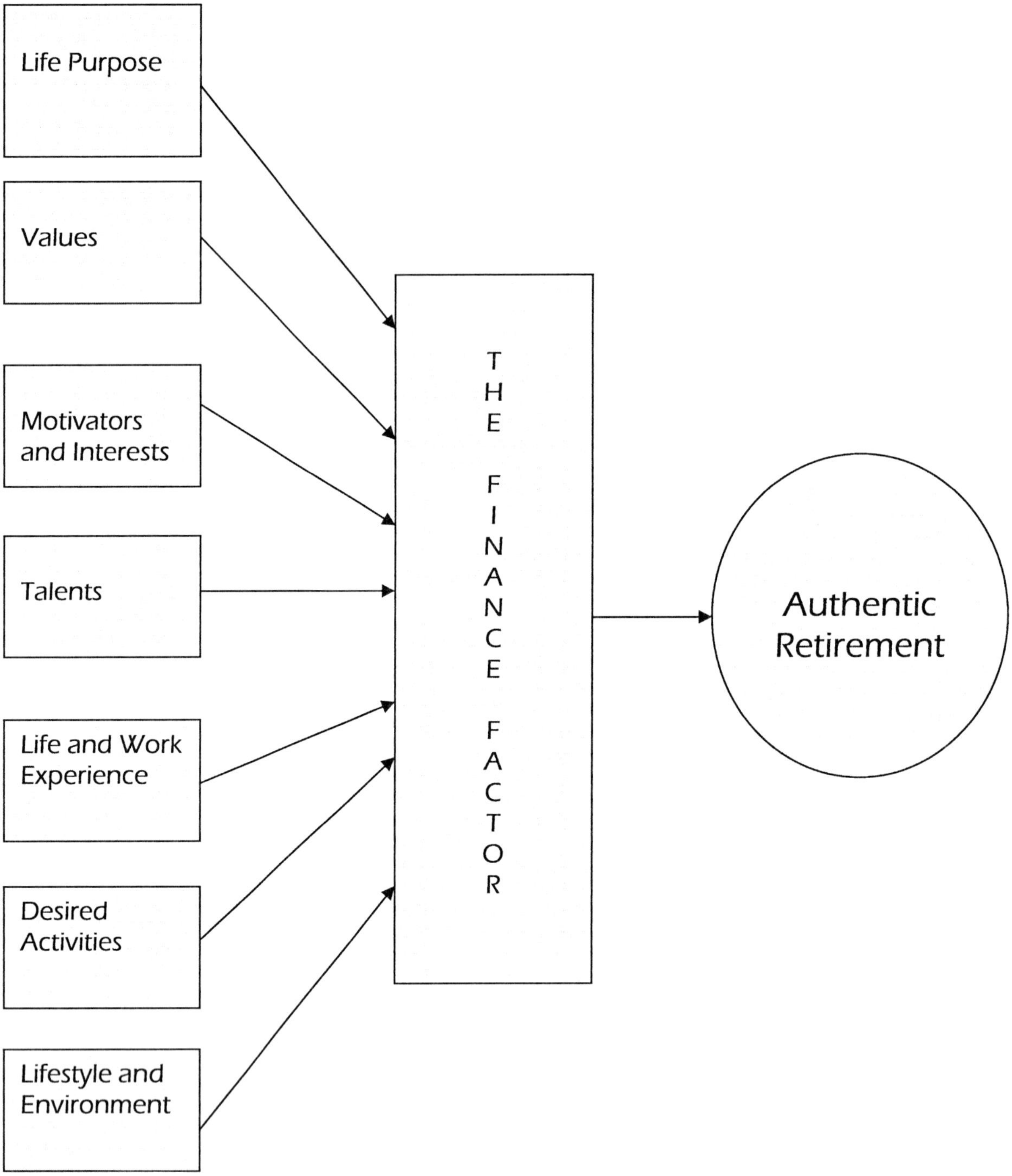

```
Life Purpose ─────────────┐
                          ↓
Values ───────────────────┐
                          ↓
Motivators and Interests ─┐
                          ↓
Talents ──────────────────→  THE FINANCE FACTOR  ──→  Authentic Retirement
                          ↑
Life and Work Experience ─┘
                          ↑
Desired Activities ───────┘
                          ↑
Lifestyle and Environment ┘
```

Coaching Authentic Retirement 29

In addition to the eight Authentic Retirement worksheets, the Ideal Retirement Exercise, Tool 2 in the Retirement Coaches Toolbox (page 141), can be used for more intuitive clients – or for those who face "analysis paralysis" using a more straightforward approach.

Case Studies

Please read the case studies below and discuss (a) whether the Authentic Retirement model is appropriate as a coaching tool with the client, (b) which factors you might emphasize first in working with them, and (c) into which of Ken Dychtwald's four groups that client might fall into: Ageless Explorers, Comfortably Contents, Live for Todays, or Sick and Tireds (see page 22 for descriptions).

1. Jerry has worked as a computer technician for most of his working life, primarily in small shop-type environments. He opened his own shop 10 years ago and serves a local market. Now age 57, he had a heart attack last year which has led him to question his values and whether or not he wants to continue working so many hours. His wife is a secretary at an insurance agency, and would like to do more traveling, both to see their grandchildren in a neighboring state as well as to explore more of the country. Their home is 90 percent paid for, and they have about $750,000 in investments and retirement plan through Jerry's company.

2. Delores is now age 62 and has worked her way up the ranks in the electric utility industry. She is now a Vice President at the local utility, where she has worked for 12 years. She is divorced and has two grown children, one of which has her own children and live nearby. She likes her work, and is in excellent physical health. Delores works out at the gym four times a week and plays golf in a ladies' group once a week. She has done extensive traveling with her work, as well as for pleasure. She has been saving toward her retirement for the last 25 years, more aggressively the past 10. She's not sure whether to retire or not, but with deregulation in the industry she feels her job may become much more demanding in the coming years.

3. Jimmy is 45 years old and just coming out of bankruptcy. He went to work for an up and coming internet firm in 1999 based on their promise of stock options and an IPO, but the company went broke in 2000 and the options became worthless. Based on his expectation of wealth, he had purchased a primary residence and a vacation home, a new Porsche, and had racked up considerable debt through lavish trips to Europe and the Pacific Rim during the internet boom. His wife left him when he lost his money, so with all the debt he had to declare bankruptcy. He doesn't really want to work that hard, especially since they share custody of their three children. Is he a candidate for Authentic Retirement?

NOTES:

KEY CONCEPTS LEARNED:

Coaching Authentic Retirement　　　　　　　　　　　　　　　　　　31

3. FINANCIAL AND LIFESTYLE ISSUES

"Money is better than poverty, if only for financial reasons."
— Woody Allen

Learning Objectives:

1. Discover the importance of our clients' beliefs about money as they affect readiness to retire, timing, and satisfaction during retirement
2. Explore ways to coach clients on the financial aspects of their retirement
3. Learn to help clients clarify options for where they live in retirement – and traps in the decision to move
4. Identify clients' attitude toward learning – and how to embrace lifelong learning

Review of Chapter 2:

1. What are some new meanings/terms for retirement?

2. How can you help your clients determine whether it's time to retire?

3. What are the elements of Authentic Retirement?

Financial Issues in Retirement Planning

Some of you reading this book or taking this course may be professional financial planners. We leave to you and your colleagues the majority of the work in this key area of retirement planning! As retirement coaches, we do not advise our clients about investments, nor do we even provide assistance in helping clients determine if their accumulated investments and assets will finance their retirement lifestyle. If your clients ask questions along this line, we recommend that first you refer them to a financial planner, and that second, as a preliminary step, you suggest that they access one or more of the free retirement calculators available on the Internet such as:

New York Life Investment Management:
http://www.nylim.com/rcg/0,2058,70_1013274,00.html

AARP:
http://sites.stockpoint.com/aarp_rc/wm/Retirement/Retirement.asp?act=LOGIN

Women's Wall Street:
http://www.womenswallstreet.com/WWS/Calculators.aspx?titleid=99

Principal Financial: http://www.principal.com/calculators/retire.htm

And the tongue-in-cheek "I Hate Financial Planning":
http://www.ihatefinancialplanning.com/homepage.jsp

For your U.S. clients to calculate their Social Security benefits:
http://www.ssa.gov/planners/calculators.htm

Most financial planners (and the typical calculator programs such as those above) assume that one needs to replace at least 80 percent of one's working income in retirement. But each situation must be considered individually! For one person, retirement may actually be *more* expensive than their work life, but for another it may be just the opposite. Senior discounts on many services and products, the absence of commuting and work-related clothing expense, smaller mortgages, the option of relocating, and a frequently lower tax bracket can lead to lower income needs for many retired clients. And with the majority of retiring Boomers anticipating working at least part-time, what they are really planning is a kind of "semi-retirement" where they will not need to depend solely on their retirement savings.

Indeed, many may need to work part-time if the level of savings of Boomers continues. The 14th Annual Retirement Confidence Survey, released April 2004 (see Resource List), found that:

> *"Despite a recovering economy and efforts to educate the population about the importance of planning and saving for retirement, the percentage of Americans who say they are saving for retirement remains stagnant."*

The study shows that 58 percent of workers say they are currently saving for retirement, but that the amount saved is low. Forty-five percent of all workers report total household assets of less than $25,000 (excluding their home). What do you suppose are some of the reasons Boomers are not saving for retirement?

Some reasons suggested in the study include:

- They think they can work long past normal retirement age
- Low expectations of how much they will need to live in retirement
- Most do not expect their standard of living to change in retirement
- Most do not know when they will be eligible for Social Security retirement benefits without a reduction for early retirement
- They are able but not willing
- The government and employers should play a bigger role

The web site http://www.choosetosave.org is recommended by this study as an information site for the general public to aid in savings education and retirement planning. Highlights of the study can be found online at http://www.ebri.org/rcs/2004/index.htm

There are also potential ethical issues in this area. We suggest adherence to the Ethical Standards of the International Coach Federation (and if you are an ICF member, compliance is required). This requires that as to the details of financial planning, we must refer our clients to other competent professionals when their needs require it (see standards 6 through 9 in Figure 4 below).

Figure 4: The ICF Standards of Ethical Conduct
http://www.coachfederation.org

Professional Conduct At Large

1) I will conduct myself in a manner that reflects well on coaching as a profession and I will refrain from doing anything that harms the public's understanding or acceptance of coaching as a profession.
2) I will honor agreements I make in my all of my relationships. I will construct clear agreements with my clients that may include confidentiality, progress reports, and other particulars.
3) I will respect and honor the efforts and contributions of others.
4) I will respect the creative and written work of others in developing my own materials and not misrepresent them as my own.
5) I will use ICF member contact information (email addresses, telephone numbers, etc.) only in the manner and to the extent authorized by the ICF.

Professional Conduct With Clients

6) I will accurately identify my level of coaching competence and I will not overstate my qualifications, expertise or experience as a coach.
7) I will ensure that my coaching client understands the nature of coaching and the terms of the coaching agreement between us.
8) I will not intentionally mislead or make false claims about what my client will receive from the coaching process or from me as their coach.

9) I will not give my clients or any prospective clients information or advice I know to be misleading or beyond my competence.
10) I will be alert to noticing when my client is no longer benefiting from our coaching relationship and would be better served by another coach or by another resource and, at that time, I will encourage my client to make that change.

Confidentiality/Privacy

11) I will respect the confidentiality of my client's information, except as otherwise authorized by my client, or as required by law.
12) I will obtain agreement with my clients before releasing their names as clients or references or any other client identifying information.
13) I will obtain agreement with the person being coached before releasing information to another person compensating me.

Conflicts of Interest

14) I will seek to avoid conflicts between my interests and the interests of my clients.
15) Whenever any actual conflict of interest or the potential for a conflict of interest arises, I will openly disclose it and fully discuss with my client how to deal with it in whatever way best serves my client.
16) I will disclose to my client all anticipated compensation from third parties that I may receive for referrals or advice concerning that client.

NOTES:

Beliefs About Money

Using a financial planner and/or financial calculator to determine how much income can be generated by a certain amount of money saved, however, does not fully address the financial aspects of retirement. There is, in fact, a "non-financial" component of finances!

Beyond the numbers themselves is our clients' beliefs about money. These can have a greater influence than one may realize on both quality of life and whether or not one's goals are achieved. The following quotation from *Spiritual Economics,* by Eric Butterworth, explains this principle:

> *"The starting point in realizing prosperity is to accept responsibility for your own thoughts, thus taking charge of your life. You are not responsible for what is said in the Wall Street Journal or what comes out of Washington*

[D.C.] in the form of economic indicators, but you are very much responsible for what you think about these things. You cannot afford to let the so-called experts decide how you are going to think and feel. For how you think and feel about the economy in general and your financial affairs in particular will unvaryingly determine what you experience."

"Even as most physical ills are now considered to be psychosomatic in origin, so we must begin to face the possibility that financial problems may be the outer manifestation of inner states of consciousness. A great idea whose time has come is that there is no such thing as a purely financial problem unrelated to false attitudes and emotions which caused it or a healthy attitude or emotion which can cure it."

Perhaps you have considered these ideas – or similar ones – as you began your coaching practice. Have you noticed a connection between your attitudes toward money, whether positive or negative, and your income?

This is an issue that we will want to explore with clients who either have seemingly unrealistic goals for retirement savings (e.g., when $1 million would do nicely, they refuse to retire until they have at least $3 million), or when the person has apparently inadequate resources and cannot seem to accumulate past a certain threshold. Indeed, clients who have too much of a focus on making and saving money as they approach retirement can compromise their enjoyment of life both while working and when they retire. At worst, retirement becomes even less satisfying than working once the drive to earn money is gone.

In a February 2004 study by the Society of Actuaries entitled "Risks of Retirement – Key Findings and Issues," financial concerns have increased substantially over the past two years. See Figure 5.

Figure 5: Retirement Concerns

Retirement Concerns	2001		2003	
	Pre-retirees	Retirees	Pre-retirees	Retirees
That you might not have enough money to pay for good health care	58%	43%	46%	79%
That you might not be able to keep the value of your savings and investments up with inflation	55%	63%	57%	78%
That you might not be able to maintain a reasonable standard of living for the rest of your (and your spouse's) life	46%	54%	46%	71%
That your spouse may not be able to maintain the same standard of living after your death, if you should die first (if married)	43%	40%	34%	47%

To further explore your clients' beliefs about money and how they may affect retirement planning, the "My Beliefs About Money" exercise, Tool 11 in the Retirement Coach's Toolbox (page 165), can be used to transform sabotaging beliefs.

Common beliefs that tend to sabotage the pre-retiree or retiree's efforts may include:

- Money doesn't grow on trees
- Money is vanity, so don't talk about it
- I'm afraid I won't have enough
- Money is hard to get, so maybe you shouldn't try
- Only the wealthy have the money
- Money is the root of all evil (a commonly misquoted Bible quotation)
- Save your money for a rainy day, don't spend it!
- Spend it all now, you may not have tomorrow!
- Money only comes to those who work hard
- The rich are evil, snobbish people
- Never act like you have more than anyone else

After reviewing the exercise in the Toolbox, fill in the opposite (and more positive) belief to each of those listed above in Figure 6, and any others your clients may identify:

Figure 6 – Sabotaging vs. Empowering Beliefs

Sabotaging Belief	Empowering Belief
Money doesn't grow on trees	Example: There is plenty of money for all of my needs and most of my desires! OR Money is a replenishable and abundant resource in my life!
Money is vanity, so don't talk about it	
I'm afraid I won't have enough	
Money is hard to get, so maybe you shouldn't try	
Only the wealthy have the money	
Money is the root of all evil	
Save your money for a rainy day, don't spend it!	
Spend it all now, you may not have tomorrow!	
Money only comes to those who work hard	
The rich are evil, snobbish people	
Never act like you have more than anyone else	

NOTES:

To Relocate or Not to Relocate?

In the old model of retirement, the goal was to pay off one's mortgage by retirement and live in the same house until health or other reasons required moving. Today, however, retirement is a time for many people to move to another house once they quit full-time work, whether near their prior residence or in another city, state, or even country. Some research shows that 45 percent of American Baby Boomers plan to move after retirement, most will stay close to home, according to Ernie Zelinski in *How to Retire Happy, Wild, and Free.* At the same time, pre-retirees and retirees recently surveyed in the *Revisioning Retirement* study (see Resource List) indicate that they value seeking personal growth and fulfillment over travel or moving to the house of their dreams:

Figure 7: Retirement Goals

Retirement Goals	Explore and tap into human potential	Travel or take vacation	Move to location of their dreams
Preretirees	81%	65%	39%
Retirees	70%	50%	35%

Retirees may choose to move for one of several reasons. Perhaps they want to be closer to grandchildren so they can be more active in their lives. Or they may desire to downsize from the home in which they raised their children to a smaller home more suitable to their new lifestyle. And others move in order to experience a new place (such as Mexico, a European country, etc.).

If you are working with clients who are considering relocating, exploring their motivations for moving can help ensure that they are not relocating for the wrong reasons. Barbara Sher points out in her book *It's Only Too Late if You Don't Start Now* that the following signs may indicate that the client is trying to "escape to freedom" – and may well find that the goal remains elusive:

- The project [or new location] is always radical, not gradual
- Clients don't debate the pros and cons of the decision
- Clients don't make plans for after the pilgrimage (because that could "jinx" the project)

In truth, she says, clients are often afraid that cautious reflection would cause them to lose courage. While there is nothing wrong with making change in retirement, the point is that if one is seeking something that can be attained and experienced in one's current circumstances, then the move may well be disappointing.

Five common mistakes clients make in choosing a retirement location, according to Dr. Warren Bland, author of *Retire in Style,* are (1) planning to retire to their summer vacation home, (2), planning to retire to the same town as their adult children, (3) planning to retire to their favorite resort town, (4), planning to retire to any place that's warm, and (5) dreaming of retiring to a golf and tennis community (but have never played either sport).

To coach clients in this situation, one powerful question can be "What does freedom mean to you?" Or, "What does moving to the south of France mean or represent to you?"

If our clients' lives have been too structured and "serious" and they long for fun, freedom and frivolousness, probing other ways they could begin to create and experience that now – perhaps postponing their planned move for three to six months until they see how this experiment goes – can help them find less drastic ways to improve their enjoyment of life. Whether it's a new hobby, some unstructured travel close to home, or starting a group of other pre-retirees around a shared interest – or just focused on being more authentic and creative! – freedom may be closer than clients think. They may still decide to move – but it will be for better reasons.

Finding Your Retirement Destination

If your client wants to move and verifies that the reasons are right, there are a number of criteria to consider. You can use the following checklist with clients to help them clarify the best place for them to live:

Element	Present (in desired location)	Absent
Climate		
Environment		
Friendliness of people		
Crime rate		
Cost of living		
Availability of public transportation		
Recreation		
Work/volunteer activities		
Health care		
Housing costs		
Cultural activities (symphony, theater, etc.)		
Continuing education opportunities		
Shopping and retail services		
Access to religious or spiritual resources		

compatible with retiree's beliefs		
Tax rates		
Air quality		

The following 10-step plan is suggested by Dr. Bland in *Retire in Style: 50 Affordable Retirement Places Across America,* (listed in Resource List) to choose a retirement location:

1. The biggest decision you must make is where you want to retire. Do you prefer something close to your present hometown or do you want to see what else is out there? Obviously your answer to this basic question can limit your search.

2. Do you want the structured and secure atmosphere of a retirement community or would you prefer a city or town with diverse groups of people, more entertainment, and wider cultural advantages?

3. Research! You can never have too many facts and statistics before making such an important move. Check books, magazines and the Internet for material you can use. Dr. Bland's book evaluates the top 50 towns and cities complete with 12 key criteria for each place. He details statistics on everything from healthcare, crime rate, climate, landscape and cost of living, even noise and air pollution. There are also maps of each place showing accessibility to the area listed.

4. Reduce your list of possible places to a manageable number, ten at most.

5. Gather additional information. Brochures, maps, economic and weather data are supplied free from chambers of commerce and tourist bureaus. Contact the local offices in the area you want to learn about.

6. Narrow your choices again, this time to five or six spots you will visit for three or four days each to get a feel of each area and general ambiance.

7. Don't rush into anything! You are moving toward a serious decision. Decide wisely and slowly, not on impulse.

8. You are close to the final cut. Eliminate all but two or three places. Visit the areas for at least three weeks each. Weigh the pros and cons carefully, including climate, cost of living and especially the people who will be your new neighbors and friends.

9. Meet with realtors and make sure the home you want is within financial reach. There are realtors who specialized in retirement living. They are called Senior Real Estate Specialists.

10. Take your time, get advice and opinions from friends and family members. But remember, the ultimate choice is yours.

For a directory of retirement communities, see this web site: http://www.retirementliving.com/RLart105.htm

One way to explore various destinations before actually moving there is by traveling in a recreational vehicle, which we discuss further in chapter 9.

NOTES:

You're Never Too Young to Learn

Another lifestyle element in retirement planning is education. Whether clients have a degree or not, or have continued learning through their professional years or not, retirement can be a great time to do so.

Remember David Stein's ideas quoted in the last chapter?:

> "The 21st century may be known as the *era of lifelong learning* and lifelong working...Retirement, the end stage of a linear working life, may be replaced with a learning, working, leisure, working, learning life cycle. In a cyclical living and working model, participating in the work force never ceases but is interspersed with periods of leisure and learning..." (emphasis added)

As new definitions of retirement emerge, whole new models of life and work are also foreshadowed. Some companies such as Intel offer paid sabbaticals for their employees, making it easier for people to alternate leisure, education and work. Perhaps as the retiree accumulates retirement assets and the need to spend most of one's waking hours generating an income decreases, it may simply be that a greater proportion of one's time can be spent taking classes, spending time with grandchildren, being with one's spouse, traveling, and doing recreational activities.

Taking classes in retirement, whether formal education or learning a hobby, tends to improve mental health as well as enjoyment and fulfillment. Community education course offerings have increased significantly in the past two decades. And the number of college students and graduates over 65 has also grown substantially. There are also over 300 lifelong learning institutes, such as the North Carolina Center for Creative Retirement http://www.unca.edu/ncccr/. Not only does taking classes in new areas enrich the individual mentally, but it puts retirees in contact with each other, thus enhancing retirees' social lives.

Users over 65 are the fastest growing segment of users of the Internet. So a class in email, basic web searching, and the like may open broad new horizons for the retiree. The 2002 AOL Roper Starch Study of Online Seniors Fifty-Five and Over found that 25 percent of retiree households were online, and that active online senior Americans averaged over 20 hours per week on the Internet. And of those seniors that are online, 93 percent report that it has improved their lives overall and 63 percent say the Internet has brought their families closer together.

One learning option for the adventurous retiree is Elderhostel, online at http://www.elderhostel.org/about/default.asp. Elderhostel is a not-for-profit organization dedicated to providing extraordinary learning adventures for people 55 and over. From New Hampshire to New Zealand, South Africa to South Dakota, Elderhostel offers its users a world of educational opportunities - at exceptional values. Prices range from $350 to $3000 or more, depending on location.

NOTES:

KEY LEARNINGS:

4. EMOTIONAL ADJUSTMENTS

> "Human beings, by changing the inner attitudes of their minds, can change the outer aspects of their lives."
> – William James

Learning Objectives:

1. Survey models for the transition process that can be used with retiring clients
2. Distinguish between "coping" and "thriving" during the retirement transition
3. Discover ways to help clients overcome fear
4. Examine the dangers of boredom and how to counter it

Review of Chapter 3:

1. What is our role as retirement coaches in our clients' financial planning for retirement?

2. What are some of the factors clients should think about if they are considering relocating when they retire?

The Nature of Transition

What do you think of when you hear the word "transition"?

Here is a working definition (from *Thriving in Transition* by Marcia Bench fka Perkins-Reed):

> "Transition is a shift from one situation or state of being to another, whether gradual or abrupt.'

Certain emotions are common when facing any transition, including retirement, such as:

- Shock (if the retirement is involuntary or unplanned)
- Denial (perhaps indicated by engaging in work-related patterns)
- Anger (at one's ex-employer or at relatives that do not understand)
- Loss (of friends from work, structure, and even youth)
- Worry, concern, fear
- Bargaining
- Guilt
- Depression
- Anxiety
- Resignation
- Acceptance
- Involvement and commitment
- Anticipation, excitement

What others come to mind?

Models of the Process

There are several current models of transition that can provide a roadmap for our clients of the shift they are making to retirement.

A. William Bridges (from the book *Transitions*). This model sees transition as being comprised of three stages:
 1) Ending
 2) Neutral zone
 3) New beginning

While this model is helpful and was one of the first developed, it has several flaws:

- It fails to address simultaneous transitions, focusing on one change at a time
- It treats transition as an isolated event, not a constant lifestyle
- The "new beginning" is not the "end" of transition – Thrivers in Dynamic Model (discussed below) continue to evaluate their choice and allow the slightest sign of discontentment or restlessness lead them to the next cycle of transition, in a cyclical pattern more appropriate for today's realities.

B . Nancy Schlossberg (from the book *Retire Smart Retire Happy*). Dr. Schlossberg, a psychologist, sees the retirement transition as having three phases, with a task to be accomplished in each:

Figure 8: Phases and Tasks of Retirement

Phase of Retirement	Tasks for Retiree	Ways to Ease the Transition
Moving out	Letting go of your work role	Name the process – grieve
Moving through	Searching for a new way to organize your life	Relabel – Retirement moratorium; Suspend decision making
Moving in	Creating your new path	Reinvest in new activities

C. Bench's Dynamic Model. A few years ago, the author did some research into the transition process as it occurs today. Often, people find themselves experiencing multiple transitions at once, much more frequently than before, and in all areas of their lives. Change is truly the only constant! The Dynamic Model of Transition illustrates the necessary phases for a complete transition:

Figure 9

The Dynamic Model of Transition
6 Phases

Phases of Transition: Evaluation, Discontentment, Crisis/Decision, Sorting Out, Vision, Action

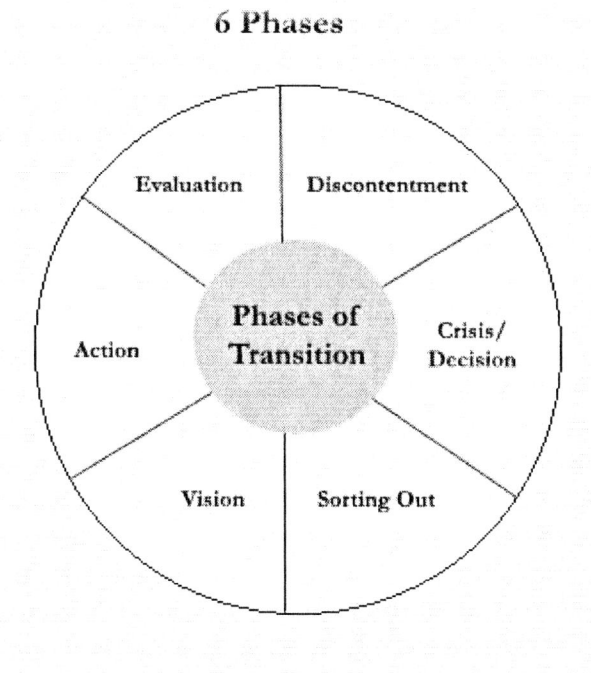

- ***Discontentment:*** a sense of dissatisfaction with the current state of affairs (e.g. job not as enjoyable as it once was, you long for the freedom of retirement, etc.)

- **Crisis/Decision:** abrupt transitions may begin with a crisis, a sudden event that forces one into transition (e.g., an early retirement eligibility announcement); gradual transitions start with discontentment and move to a *decision to change* – an unwillingness to allow things to continue the way they were

- **Sorting Out:** a period of confusion, as though we have lost our bearings, in which we reflect on our values, purpose and choices, try on new possibilities, and experience a roller-coaster of emotions

- **Vision:** a mental picture of the next steps (e.g., the lifestyle we want to pursue or the kind of retirement we want to experience)

- **Action:** we begin our retirement planning in earnest – perhaps deciding on a retirement date, discussing possibilities with our spouse, deciding where we might want to move, calculating our financial resources, and the like. And ultimately we retire. But we don't stop there!

- **Evaluation:** periodic questioning, as objectively as we can, as to whether our retirement (or other situation to which we have transitioned) is still serving us and allowing us to optimize our potential, or whether we need to refine it a bit (or a lot!)

Note that a person can be at different phases regarding each of several transitions he/she may be experiencing at a given time.

D. William Sadler. In the book *The Third Age: 6 Principles for Growth and Renewal After 40,* Dr. William Sadler illustrates the conventional paradigm of the life cycle as a sideways "S" curve. Our education and preparation to begin our career are represented by the downward curve, then the upward trend is starting and raising a family and our primary working years. Then, the rest of our life is "downhill," a time of decline.

Ideally, instead of that strictly downward momentum, our life will look more like overlapping cycles, such that we still have the growth into and through our career, but at mid-career we begin another overlapping curve as we envision and begin to plan our "third age" – or retirement. That part of our lives continues in an upward curve until the very end of our lives.

E. Business Psychology Research Institute. In the article "The Psychology of Retirement: How to Cope Successfully with a Major Life Transition," by The Everyday Psychologist, Denial, Depression, Anger and Acceptance are given as the four stages of retirement. Several factors are mentioned as predictors of whether one will "succeed" or "fail" at retirement. They include such things as health status, financial status, whether the person retired early, social support network, and others discussed in this book. This 57-page e-book can be purchased at the following link: http://store.yahoo.com/bpri/psycofrethow.html

NOTES:

"Coper" and "Thriver" Approaches to Facing Transition

When facing a transition, clients have a choice as to whether they will welcome it or resist it. Those who resist we call "Copers," and those who embrace "Thrivers." We discuss in this section the traits of each, and you can use the Coper/Thriver Quiz, Tool 12 in the Retirement Coaches Toolbox (page 167), to help clients determine which best describes them.

Coping

A "Coper" is someone who resists change; it is a defensive, reactive strategy, not a proactive one. And while the common use of the term "to cope" is to attempt to overcome problems and difficulties (which may not sound too bad), its primary definition in the dictionary is to "maintain a contest or combat." So Coping literally puts one at war with change, rather than living peacefully with it. Copers share 10 characteristics:

1. **Need for control:** Copers need to believe they are in charge of their lives – including the other people in their life! – and when faced with transition try to resolve it as quickly as possible. This is not always the best approach when one is facing a life or career crossroads which requires reflection and slowing down. As the author of *Thriving in Transition* states it, "Manipulation of externals is a Coper response to an unmanageable internal experience."
2. **Mistrust, suspicion:** Copers mistrust everything and are overly skeptical; this causes them to believe that life and other people are fundamentally "against" them and that they must constantly be on the defensive to avoid being taken advantage of.
3. **Disconnected from spirituality**: Most Copers, even those that attend a church or synagogue, are fundamentally disconnected from their innate sense of spirituality. When a crisis or major life transition such as retirement occurs, they lack spiritual roots from which to draw support and feel particularly "lost" and adrift, as though they have lost their bearings.

4. **No sense of purpose:** To Copers, life is just a series of daily experiences without a thread to tie them together or a purpose for living. They have either not succeeded in finding a purpose (if they have looked for it), or the important life questions about purpose have not yet occurred to them. This leads to a sense of emptiness and dissatisfaction that is intensified during retirement.
5. **Victim thinking, blaming:** Flowing directly from purposelessness is the tendency to blame others for one's lot in life and to see oneself as a victim. The government, one's upbringing or parents, one's boss, or other external source is to blame for what is wrong in one's life and work – and therefore one is powerless to change it. Another way to say it: they have an external (vs. internal) locus of control.
6. **Disconnected from feelings:** Copers have not developed a vocabulary of the heart; they will usually answer "fine" when asked how they are, and either don't know how to or are not willing to share their true experience. They become dulled not only to the pain of life, but also to the joy that is available.
7. **Rigid thinking:** Copers are usually black-and-white thinkers. Prejudices and stereotypes are used commonly, and everything is either one way or the other; no shades of gray. Such systems of thinking, rigid as they are, are destined to decay and die – vitality and fresh ideas can no longer enter the system.
8. **Negative attitudes:** Most Copers are classic pessimists: the glass is always half empty. Copers' negative beliefs about life – even if based in fact – become self-fulfilling prophecies. They believe things will go badly and they do.
9. **No healthy support system:** Some Copers are loners and have no support system at all; but still others surround themselves with other rigid-thinking, negative people who are disconnected from their feelings so that they can commiserate about their lot in life.
10. **Lack of balance:** Finally, Copers are often lopsided in their energy invested in work versus personal life – they may be overachieving workaholics or they may be seen as lazy, but in any even they have a skewed sense of priorities. This continues into retirement.

Thriving

To "thrive" is to grow vigorously; to flourish. Using the analogy of a thriving plant can bring to mind the vision of ourselves with a vibrant ability to deal with transition, blooming brightly and bursting with life. Being a Thriver is akin to what has been described as a "peak performer" by Abraham Maslow and Charles Garfield (author of the book *Peak Performers)* and other similar description; however, this profile is specifically derived from Marcia Bench's research over several years of the traits that are necessary to handle *transition* (and in turn retirement) effectively. Thrivers share six clusters of traits:

- Attentiveness

- Groundedness
- Trust
- Proactive Purpose
- Optimistic Confidence
- Systems Thinking

Let's look at each of these in detail, with the specific traits that comprise each:

1. **Attentiveness:** paying attention to what happens in both the individual's internal and external environment
    a. **Self-Awareness:** Thrivers continually strive to learn more about themselves and to be aware of how they are feeling, and what messages their inner self is communicating.
    b. **Commitment to growth:** Pursuing personal growth and expanding themselves in ever-new ways are priorities for Thrivers.
    c. **Internal motivation:** Unlike Copers, Thrivers have an *internal* locus of control: they initiate needed changes in their lives, and they do not allow external circumstances to dictate their emotional state.
    d. **Receptivity to new experiences**: In contrast to the rigid thinking of Copers, Thrivers are open to new ideas and withhold judgment until they have had an opportunity to experience or evaluate the idea or activity.

2. **Groundedness:** a three-legged stool with the following three "legs" which, when all are strong, provide a firm foundation for dealing with anything life metes out
    a. **Spirituality:** Thrivers are connected first with something larger than themselves; it may be a traditional religious practice or church, or it may be nature, ritual, or alternative philosophy. This spiritual connection provides both comfort and context for the transition experience.
    b. **Support system:** In addition, Thrivers surround themselves with a healthy support system of other Thrivers who share victories and defeats, transitions and new beginnings. This may consist of family, friends, co-workers, fellow church members, or a smattering of all of these.
    c. **Resilience:** The third leg is inner resilience: literally, the ability to bounce back from adversity. Some Thrivers have a tendency toward this trait from birth; others develop it in the "school of hard knocks." But they are less paralyzed by even the most unexpected transition because they know they can rely on their developed ability to bounce back.

3. **Trust:** the ability to relax into the transition process, based on a knowingness that the process is unfolding just as it should; they do not need to have a rigid

model of how things will be (note that this is the opposite of the Copers' tendency towards mistrust, suspicion, blame and victim-thinking)

    a. **Willing to feel:** Realizing that as human beings we are designed to feel a wide range of emotions, Thrivers relish each emotion and learn how to express them in appropriate ways. They also see their strong feelings as messengers to show them what issues are ripe for exploration now.

    b. **Comfortable with ambiguity:** Ambiguity – or uncertainty and "in-betweenness" – is an integral part of transition. Thrivers have learned how to continue to be productive, to attend to their personal development, and to integrate the new options as they emerge. Therefore, the "in-between" stage does not intimidate or stop Thrivers.

    c. **Trust their own process of growth**: Thrivers trust that each of the elements which disrupted the way things were will be resolved in the right time and manner for them – and their unique style and needs. They feel less need to compare themselves with others because of this trait.

    d. **Self-nurturing:** Thrivers recognize that if they don't allow self-nurturing a place in daily life, they will become depleted and less effective. They determine what nurtures them (massage, yoga, exercise – popular with all Thrivers interviewed! – golf, meditation or nature) and regularly engage in those activities.

4. **Proactive Purpose:** a trait cluster which combines a sense of purpose with the ability and willingness to make choices proactively – vs. reactively – to optimize one's quality of life in all areas

    a. **Sense of purpose:** Thrivers have asked themselves the question, "What is my purpose in life?" and have found an answer. See chapters 2 and 6 for some tools to help clients with this issue.

    b. **Dreaming beyond practical**: Thrivers refuse to be limited by small thinking or what has been done before. They dream big and test their own limits. And they often achieve outstanding results through this process!

    c. **Proactive creation:** An 8-step process outside the scope of this book by which the Thriver clearly envisions a desired result or scenario, refuses to be stopped by apparent setbacks, stays open to surprising results through the principle of "synchronicity," and moves confidently toward his/her desired results.

5. **Optimistic Confidence:** unflappable optimism and confidence, born not from having the right genes but through achieving early small successes and building on that foundation to achieve more and more of what the Thriver wants in life

    a. **Self-confidence:** Thrivers' self-assurance, developed over time, builds from confidence in familiar situations to an openness to the unknown.

    b. **Playful risk-taking**: Thrivers view life as a game to be played, not a problem to be solved. This allows them to take so-called "risks" when called for, but it does not elicit as much fear in Thrivers as others.

    c. **Optimism**: Thrivers' decide, or tend, to expect the best possible outcome from an event, knowing that things will work out for the best – even when it doesn't look that way right now! Martin Seligman's research, as outlined in the book *Learned Optimism,* documents that this trait can be learned – one need not be born with it.

    d. **Flexible adapting**: Like the plant that changes its structure to grow in a difficult place, such as between two rocks, Thrivers are adept at modifying their habits as well as their thought patterns to integrate the changes life presents. They are not so wedded to one belief system or way of thinking that they cannot change when a situation demands it, or when they find something they prefer.

6. **Systems Thinking**: ability to see the big picture and the interrelationships between the elements of each system

    a. **Systems perspective:** Thrivers have a perspective by which they recognize that each element of their lives, as well as each system within the world, are interdependent. That is, action taken in one dimension or system affects the others as well. *Example:* choosing to retire and move to another state will also affect one's spouse's emotional health, one's opportunities to visit, time with grandchildren, cost of living, clothing needed, etc.

    b. **Interactive experimentation:** Our Western culture is oriented to judge each experience and to label it as "good" or "bad," "success" or "failure." This just contributes to rigid, dualistic thinking. Thrivers, by contrast, view life as a scientist does his laboratory: it is a place to experiment and to learn from the results. If the results are not what he had hoped, a scientist does not give up (nor does a Thriver). Instead, he evaluates what happened, makes course corrections or changes, and tries again. This is the Thriver's attitude toward pursuing new options.

    c. **Humor:** Since life is a game to Thrivers, they learn to laugh at themselves and their foibles. Humor stimulates a healthier immune system, according to recent research. And it makes life more fun!

    d. **Balance:** Thrivers know that overworking or overdoing anything will cause their primary relationship and family relationships to get out of balance, and vice versa. So they continually re-evaluate their priorities and strive for balance among the changing elements in their lives.

See the Retirement Coach's Toolbox Tool 13 (page 170) for a list of coaching questions to help clients develop each cluster of the Thriver personality.

NOTES:

Applying the Coper/Thriver Approaches

Please discuss:

1: Jean, age 35, married John 15 years ago. Jean moved directly from her parents' home to her husband's home, and they began a family right away. She didn't work in the early years, when the children were young, but now that they're beginning high school, she has felt for a long time that she wanted to go back to school and prepare for a career. Despite objections from John, who is retired, she began classes two nights a week six months ago. John has done nothing but complain since then, and is not willing to help with the housework, shuttling the children to their various events, and meal preparation. "That's my wife's job," he claims.

What would Jean's response to the situation be if she were a Coper?

If she were a Thriver?

2: Bob, now age 47, took an early retirement package last week from his job as a systems analyst with ComputerWhiz on short notice. He has been with ComputerWhiz for 18 years, in progressively more responsible positions. His first career was as a fifth grade math teacher, after which he received his master's degree and began work at ComputerWhiz. He doesn't want to teach math any more, and has no other job or career plans (other than a little savings toward his retirement) since he enjoyed his systems analyst job tremendously. However, he is an avid sports fisherman and has developed a series of rather unique lures that all of his friends rave about.

What would Bob's response to the situation be if he were a Coper?

If he were a Thriver?

Overcoming Fear

It is not unusual for our clients to encounter fear as they approach retirement. . They may ask themselves questions like:

- What will this new lifestyle be like?
- Will I like it?
- What if I retire after looking forward to it for years and then "fail" at it?

What most people tend to do when faced with fear is either resist it or try to ignore it, hoping it will go away. But it often doesn't! What happens instead is that the fear occupies a lot of people's mental energy and distracts them from their daily activities – and may even result in clients' postponing retirement just to eliminate the uncomfortable feeling!

Often, simply asking the client, "What are you afraid of?" and having them face the worst case scenario can significantly reduce the fear. Susan Jeffers' book, *Feel the Fear and Do It Anyway,* is a helpful reference for reluctant clients. In fact, we encourage you to take your clients even further than that: embrace the fear! You might ask a question such as "What if this fear were a friend – what would it want you to know?" Or "What is the message in the fear?" Or have them write a dialogue between the "voice of fear" and the "voice of confidence" to flesh out inner messages.

Since fear is merely an indicator that clients are outside their "comfort zone" of familiar experience, gaining more information about the feared event (here, retirement) often helps clients feel more comfortable with their decisionmaking. Books such as those listed in the Resource List at the end of this manual and other articles and web sites can provide this needed information for clients.

We can also remind our clients that their body and mind are wise and that they normally won't feel fear unless there is some good reason for it. Rather than let it stop them, they can face it, have a dialogue with it, and understand the message it wants them to hear. After having considered the best case/worst case scenarios, they can then make their decision about whether to move forward into the unfamiliar action step or transition that the fear has warned them about.

NOTES:

Dangers of Boredom

Some retirees find that living in the "lap of leisure" is not what they expected! "Indeed, one study showed that approximately a quarter of all North American retirees are unhappy because they would rather be working. Almost a third of retirees return to work sooner or later; most do so within a year of retiring." (Zelinski, Ernie, *How to Retire Happy, Wild and Free*).

While being bored may not sound like a large problem, in fact boredom is at the root of many psychological conditions retirees experience. If the retiree cannot find a way around it, it can devolve into depression, extreme loneliness, and even death.

When clients come to us who are feeling bored with their retirement lifestyle – or even better, present that concern *before* they retire – we can offer such ideas as these:

- Encourage clients to develop leisure interests and/or hobbies while still working so they can spend even more time doing them in retirement if desired.
- Retire gradually! Similarly to entrepreneurs starting a part-time business while employed by someone else and eventually quitting their job to pursue their business full-time, retirees can, over a period of even years, devote an increasing proportion of their time to non-work activities. Zelinski suggests that we never actually commit to retirement in the traditional sense of the word, but instead think of ourselves as "reorienting our lives."
- Volunteer or work part-time to maintain the stimulation that comes from interacting with others and being part of something.
- Explore new venues for leisure activities. From exercise to spending time with a neighbor or the neighbor's children, jewelry-making to singing in a community choir, there are endless activities to fill one's time when work is no longer a required element. (More on this in chapter 9!)

NOTES:

Case Study:

Renee is 59 years old. She was married to a business man who successfully climbed the corporate ladder. She served in a variety of positions in support of his career. She was a wonderful social hostess, fund raiser, served on many community organizational boards and participated in numerous volunteer activities. She made several geographical moves with her husband's promotions and raised two children. After 22 years they had attained a very comfortable lifestyle and retirement was just thought to be a normal progression within the next five years. However, the marriage then began to deteriorate. When her children went off to college, Renee decided to enroll in some college courses herself. She enjoyed learning and went on the complete a degree and certification in a field she enjoyed.

As the marriage ended, Renee found herself needing to take a part-time job as she no longer had any funds available for retirement or her former lifestyle. She considered herself too old to compete with other applicants in her fields of interest, and became angry as interview after interview produced a "thanks but no thanks" letter. The future looked pretty bleak to Renee.

How would Renee's reluctance likely appear?

Is she a Coper or a Thriver?

Would Renee be coachable? Why or why not?

KEY CONCEPTS LEARNED:

5. WORK ISSUES

"The world is full of willing people, some willing to work, the rest willing to let them."
– Robert Frost

Learning Objectives:

1. Explore how to help clients decide whether or not to continue working in retirement
2. Become aware of numerous work options and work substitutes for clients
3. Examine age discrimination against retirees and pre-retirees
4. Learn how different generations interact in the workplace
5. Discover how to help clients in the "Traditional" generation adopt a Self-Employed Mindset

Review of Chapter 4:

1. What are some of the current models for the transition process that can be used with retiring clients?

2. What is the difference between "coping" and "thriving" during the retirement transition?

3. How can you help your clients overcome their fear about retiring?

4. What are the dangers of boredom in retirement?

To Work or Not to Work, that is the Question

People who retired within the more traditional model of retirement typically did not even consider working during retirement – that would be an oxymoron! But today, for all of the reasons discussed in chapters 1 and 2, some kind of work or other gainful activity is a desirable option for a large percentage of retirees. You will recall that almost half of the nearly 70 percent of workers in the 2003 AARP survey who have not yet retired envision working into their 70's or beyond.

Many people's primary motivation to work during their primary working years is to make money. Work choices in retirement, however, are often based on other reasons such as the following top five reasons for working in retirement, according to the AARP survey:

1. Desire to stay mentally active (83%)
2. Desire to stay physically active (80%)
3. Desire to remain productive or useful (76%)
4. Desire to do something fun or enjoyable (66%)
5. You'll need the health benefits (56%) tied with Desire to help other people (also 56%)

Note that making extra money is not in that list! For that reason, the first seven factors of the Authentic Vocation™ Model of Career Development can be particularly useful for retirees planning their work. Those factors (which echo the Authentic Retirement™ Model discussed in chapter 2 for planning one's overall retirement lifestyle) are:

1. **Life purpose:** what is the purpose or mission of your life that *must* be expressed through your work?
2. **Values:** what values must be expressed in your work for optimal satisfaction?
3. **Motivators:** what motivates you to do your best?
4. **Skills:** what skills do you have that you want to continue using?
5. **Work Experience:** what experience can you leverage in your next position?
6. **Desired Job/Career:** what job titles and/or industries would suit your goals?
7. **Environment:** what location, culture, and other factors would be critical in your work environment?
8. **Business Reality:** Is your target financially viable? Can you make a living at it? If not, what needs to be adjusted so you can?

To explore these factors in detail with your clients, we recommend using the workbook *Discover Your Authentic Vocation* by Marcia Bench with them, available through Career Coach Institute (see Resource List).

So how can we help our clients decide whether working during retirement is right for them? The questionnaire, "Should I Work in Retirement?," Tool 14 in the Retirement Coaches Toolbox (page 172), can help.

NOTES:

Work Options for Retired/Retiring Clients

Retirement can be a time to finally explore a passion that was not financially feasible earlier, to create a nonprofit organization, to serve as a mentor or substitute grandparent for a child who has none. The options are as limitless as the creativity of the client and his/her coach! Some include:

- Keeping current job
- Working part-time at prior job
- Changing careers
- Taking a sabbatical
- Becoming an entrepreneur (traditional or so-called "social entrepreneur")
- Mentoring
- Contract or temporary work
- Pursue a work substitute (e.g. volunteering)

Keeping Current Job

Some clients may consider themselves "retired" but still want to work – perhaps mentoring and training a future replacement or doing work that is not quite as demanding as before. Less than 44 percent of those surveyed in the 2000 Cornell Retirement and Well-Being Study (see Resource List), stated that full-time work was their preference.

Pros:

- Possibilities for better salary and benefits are greater – clients will not have to start over as they might in a new career at the bottom of the ladder.
- Flexible scheduling may be an option.
- Usually includes fringe benefit package (including health insurance)
- It is familiar.
- Clients do not have to risk age discrimination in a job search.

Cons:

- Could lead to boredom if clients are not enjoying the work.
- Employer could take clients for granted.
- An early retirement offer may be too good to pass up, so even if they desire to continue working, the company has the option to ask them to leave.

Working Part-Time At Prior Job

Clients who want to reduce the number of hours they work – or retire in stages or more gradually – may choose to negotiate a part-time work arrangement with their former employer. Almost half of preretirees surveyed in the Cornell Study stated that they would like to reduce their work hours.

Pros:

- Extends time for retirees to adjust to retirement before quitting work altogether (if that is their plan)
- Flexible scheduling is more likely
- Gives clients more time to pursue hobbies and spend time with family and friends
- Lowers stress level, thereby improving health in many cases
- Continues the positive aspects of ongoing employment
- Could result in continued fringe benefits (e.g., health insurance)

Cons:

- Many companies do not offer benefits to part-time workers below a certain number of hours
- Prior position may not lend itself to part-time employment, or employer may not be open to the idea

Changing Careers

Whether clients are bored with their prior career or simply feel that now is the time to try something new, a career change at retirement can feel like a new "lease on life" when more fulfilling work results.

Pros:

- Can result in improved work satisfaction
- Sometimes brings increased compensation
- Renews zest and vigor about life
- Validates self-esteem

Cons:

- Clients will need to thoroughly examine various aspects of their ideal work and determine the best option(s) for them.

- Clients may have to start at the bottom of the ladder, with reduced salary, less prestige and other offsetting consequences.
- It is frustrating and time–consuming to look for a new job.
- They may face age discrimination.
- Employers may be reluctant to hire them if they lack experience in the field.
- It will usually require a refresher course on current job search techniques.

Taking a Sabbatical

If clients are not ready to quit work yet but want a break from it, or desire to study abroad or travel as a "trial retirement," or for other reasons, a sabbatical can provide such an opportunity. Whether paid or unpaid, these breaks from traditional work to travel, study, or pursue other interests can range in length from a few weeks to a full year. Some companies offer paid sabbaticals after a certain number of years of service. Two references on this topic are included in the Resource List.

Pros:

- A sabbatical can provide an opportunity to try out retirement.
- It could give clients a chance to return to school to update skills and knowledge or learn a new trade.
- They will have time to travel or explore other interests and hobbies.

Cons:

- They might jeopardize their job if their employer doesn't miss them during their absence!
- This is not a good option if clients love their job and do not want to be away from it.

Becoming an Entrepreneur – Traditional or Social

Increasingly, retirees are choosing to own their own business, whether full-time or part-time, home-based or not, traditional business or a so-called social entrepreneur focus. More than 50 percent of all small businesses are owned by people age 50 or over.

Pros:

- Being an entrepreneur could fulfill a lifelong dream.
- The business could become very profitable.
- Clients may enjoy the flexibility of being their own boss.
- The Internet offers seniors many business opportunities not previously available.
- Entrepreneurship can be very rewarding.

Cons:

- It takes a significant amount of time, energy and enthusiasm to be a successful entrepreneur.
- Being an entrepreneur may not be appropriate for every client (see below)
- Clients may need to learn or develop business skills that they do not yet possess

So-called "social entrepreneurship," a term coined by Mark Freedman in *Prime Time: How Baby Boomers Will Revolutionize Retirement and Transform America,* refers to people who are creating new institutions that "reinvent retirement by reimagining society." That is, they are developing organizations to replace some of the institutions that hold people back from their goals with new ones that may serve them well in the future. One example is Hope Meadows, an innovative living community in which adults age 56 and older receive reduced rent in spacious apartments in return for volunteering to help young people in residence as "honorary grandparents." Samaritan House, Volunteers in Medicine, and Troops to Teachers are other examples discussed in the book.

For a thorough treatment of the options of business ownership, see "The Five Roads to Self-Employment" (see Resource List).

In addition, various entrepreneurial assessments may help clients decide whether or not entrepreneurship is for them:

http://midcareer.monster.com/tools/self_employment/
http://www.liraz.com/webquiz.htm

And the Retirement Coaches Toolbox also contains an Entrepreneurial Quiz as Tool 15 (page 173).

Mentoring

One of the benefits of reaching retirement age (whatever that is today!) is that people have usually developed valuable expertise from which others can benefit. Sharing that knowledge through a mentoring arrangement, or passing on what one has learned as part of a succession planning initiative within a company, can be a win-win-win arrangement for retiree, employee and company.

Pros:

- Mentoring can be personally rewarding.
- Company retains intellectual capital that would otherwise be lost.
- Offers retiree an avenue through which to seamlessly leave his/her position.
- Can generate additional income unless done in volunteer capacity.

Cons:

- Can lead to assumption that retiree is leaving the company (which is fine unless they do not want to!).
- Is only suitable for individuals who are patient and good teachers/coaches.

Contract or Temporary Work

Knowing that many retirees desire a more flexible lifestyle, contract work (where one is paid by the hour, usually to complete a project) or temporary work (working through an agency that matches qualified individuals with assignments of one day to several months in length, paying the individual directly for his/her work) can be very viable options.

Pros:

- Flexible scheduling
- Variety of assignments can be interesting!
- Retiree can accept or refuse assignments, and take breaks for as much as weeks at a time
- Provides supplemental income
- Some temporary agencies offer fringe benefits to workers after meeting a threshold of hours worked

Cons:

- Agency/company is usually not obligated to provide any minimum number of hours' or days' work for an individual, so if retiree is counting on this for income it is not as dependable as part-time work with set hours
- Age discrimination can enter into this process too

Pursue a Work Substitute

The "Ageless Explorers" and "Comfortably Contents" (see page 22), who have been saving for retirement for some time and are financially secure now, may have no interest in working for a wage. Nevertheless, they want an outlet through which they can experience achievement, contribution, and/or gainful activity. Volunteering or other substitutes for work can satisfy these needs. Nearly half of the retirees surveyed in the Cornell Study were involved in volunteering.

Pros:

- Meets one's motivational needs that are now more important than money
- Offers value to the community, association, or other venue in which they serve
- Allows them to pursue an interest, cause or value that it was not financially viable to pursue while working

Cons:

- Can become as time-consuming as work!
- While it meets mental/emotional needs, it does not provide any financial remuneration
- Can take time away from time with family and friends

NOTES:

Age Discrimination and Retirement

Many older workers believe that they are discriminated against in their job search on the basis of age. An article on the AARP web site written by Sally James, Executive Director of Career Encores, a non-profit corporation that links employers with job seekers 50 years and older in Southern California, addresses this point. "Make Age Irrelevant by Beating Negative Views" (see Resource List) suggests that one's attitude can greatly influence one's job search results. What job seekers think about themselves and what many employers think about older workers can create formidable obstacles.

Some negative attitudes among older workers might include:

- Older workers are not welcome in the workplace
- I'm too old to start a new career
- I know more than the young people interviewing me

But it is not just job seeker attitudes that are at fault; employers also sometimes hold negative views! Representative employer attitudes include:

- I don't want to hire anyone over 60
- This person seems overqualified

- I want to hire older people because they are cheaper
- This person may retire soon - why should I hire him/her?

How would you counter these negative views?

Figure 10: Overcoming Negative Attitudes

Negative Attitude	Alternative or Strategy to Overcome
Employee:	
Older workers are not welcome in the workplace	
I'm too old to start a new career	
I know more than the young people interviewing me	
Employer:	
I don't want to hire anyone over 60	
This person seems overqualified	
I want to hire older people because they are cheaper	
This person may retire soon - why should I hire him/her?	

Making age irrelevant is critical for the older job seeker, but Sally James described one employer who likes to hire older workers. This employer said, "I like to hire your people because they come in on Monday and they have not been surfing all weekend. Surfers never come in on Monday." This kind of thinking, however, might be changing. According to Sally, "We have an increasing number of older surfers in Southern California."

For tips on finding a post-retirement job, we recommend http://www.notyetretired.com/section.php?id=5

Following are some recruiters who specialize in placing retirees:

http://www.seniors4hire.org/
http://www.seniorjobbank.com/
http://www.retiredbrains.com/
http://www.careerencores.org

NOTES:

The Importance of a Self-Employed Mindset

The so-called self-employed mindset is a new way of thinking about work. Possessing a self-employed mindset means that each of us is in charge of our own career. This concept is totally foreign to "Traditionals." They see themselves as *working for a company* and not as *working for themselves.*

> *"Always view yourself as self-employed. The biggest mistake that you can ever make in life is to think that you work for anybody else but yourself. You are self-employed; you are the president of your own personal services corporation."*
> -Brian Tracy

Compare this mindset with the older "employed/dependent" mindset in the comparison which follows:

Employed/Dependent	**Self-Employed/Independent**
Company will change; they are to blame for what's wrong in my work	*I will change; self-responsibility for career satisfaction*

("I am in charge of my work and life no matter what the economy, no matter whether I work inside or outside the traditional workplace.")

Ignore my fears	*Face my fears*

(Fears might include "I don't know what I'd do if I lost my job," "I wouldn't know how to do/find another job." "What if my retirement money doesn't last as long as I live?" "No one will want to hire me because of my age." "I am overqualified." "I am nothing without my work.")

Company will take care of me	*I will be myself and collaborate with others*

("I can be independent, in charge of my career, and at the same time be interdependent by working in collaboration with others and contributing to others.")

*Work **for** company, do what's*	***Join** company, provide excellent*

expected   *service*

("I voluntarily offer my services to others through my organization, and my organization supports me in that project.")

Rest on my laurels   *Commit to continuous learning*

("Being a lifelong learner helps me to keep current in my field.")

"Just doing a job."   *Creating meaningful work*

("I experience self-fulfillment when I express myself and make a difference through my work. It is satisfying to be able to make a living at what is most personally meaningful.")

      (Chart Adapted from *We are All Self-Employed* by Cliff Hakim)

The self-employed mindset can be summarized in a "contract" one makes with oneself, such as the sample below:

Figure 11: Sample Self-Employment Contract

I have a day- to- day contract with my company to use my services. When the contract is no longer mutually beneficial, I will look for other opportunities, rather than waiting for "them" to change. I acknowledge that there is no more "they." I choose to see myself as the major player in my relationship with my employer. I will negotiate rather than accept and placate. I will tell the truth as I see it about my needs and interests, rather than trying to fit into other's expectations of where my career should go.

I will continually test out my marketable skills by interviewing for other jobs. When people ask me, "What do you do?" I will not let myself off the hook by simply responding with the name of my prestigious company. Instead, I will say what I do and teach people about my skills. I will put who I currently work for in the proper perspective.

You can use this example with your clients and suggest that they write their own Self-Employment Contract as they learn to adopt this mindset.

Author Cliff Hakim asks his clients four questions to help them adopt a new attitude about work:

1. What do you really want?
2. What do you bring to others?
3. What will others buy from you?
4. Who's the boss?

Describe the application of the self-employed mindset in retirement planning. How can/should your clients use it?

NOTES:

Generational Issues at Work

"Traditionals" is a term used to describe those people born between 1920 and 1943 grew up in a time when one expected to work for life at one job or at least to work for the same company for life. This generation was loyal to its employers and believed that in return the company would "take care of them."

Look at Figure 12 on page 70. Focusing just on the Traditionals column first, how would this generation's formative experiences and orientations create (a) assets and (b) liabilities as they approach retirement?

Examining the beliefs of the "Traditional" and "Boomer" categories together will help us to understand why it may be difficult for them to change to a self-employed mindset. Revisit Figure 12, looking now at *all* columns, especially Traditionals and Boomers (since they are either at or approaching retirement age). Would the self-employed mindset come easily or hard to Boomers? Why/why not?

What barriers can you anticipate as these two generations interact?

Opportunities?

Case Study:

Frank is sixty years old and has worked for ABC Company for 25 years. Frank is the company's Chief Financial Officer and is well qualified for his position. ABC Company has recently been sold and new management has taken over. The new management style is in conflict with Frank's values and beliefs concerning how people should be treated and how the business should be run. On several occasions his advice to management has been ignored. Early retirement packages have been offered to Frank and others who have longevity of 20 years or more with the company. Even if Frank takes the offer he believes he will need to continue working for financial reasons. However, he is afraid that he will not be able to find a job elsewhere due to his age.

What barriers, internal and external, are keeping Frank as one of the employed/dependent?

What opportunities does he have to become independent/self-employed?

NOTES:

KEY CONCEPTS LEARNED:

Figure 12: SHAPERS OF GENERATIONAL DIFFERENCES

Reprinted with Permission from Janine Moon, PCCC http://www.cpcoaching.com

SHAPERS	TRADITIONAL	BABY BOOMERS	GENERATION X	GENERATION Y /NEXTER
Born:	(1920-1943)	(1943-1960)	(1961-1980)	(1981-)
Defining moments/ history	World War II; post-war boom; Korean War; New Deal; silver screen; labor unions; golden age of radio	Civil rights; TV; Vietnam War; "causes;" Sex, Drugs, Rock & Roll; political assassinations; cold war	Global economy; MTV; AIDS; technology; Challenger; changed family values; Watergate	Technologically sophisticated; World Trade Center attack; internet chat; Oklahoma City
Economics	Depression-era beliefs; 50s, 60s, 70s good times; Fortune 500 CEOs	Money important; workaholics; career first, family second; yuppies; 2- income families	Rapid domestic declines and downturns; rapid movement to global economy	Highs and lows; protected by parents; limited global barriers
Common Experiences	"Keepers of the Grail;" loyalty; patriotism; Gray Panthers / AARP	Many career choices, options; empowerment; diversity; personal gratification; soul searching	Highly educated; techno-savvy; divorced families; two-income families; latch key kids	Street smart; achievement oriented; instant feedback and rewards (video games)
Work Ethic	Loyal; dependable; stick-to-it-ness; labor hard; one job/company for life; Depression-raised; duty before pleasure	Yuppies; workaholics; career first, family second; hard work is rewarded; can have it all; later BBs, cynical	Understand no guarantee; skills oriented; don't buy "can have it all;" informal; me-focused; pragmatic; life balance important	Heroic spirit; confident; achievement-oriented; value diversity; desire constructive feedback; stricter moral code
Career expectations	Any job; find work, keep it	Get better job than Dad; move up the ladder	Focus on journey, skill building; redefine "better	Work that matters and provides on-going learning;

				than Dad"	use newest technologies
Leadership style / work motivators	Directive style; logical; SOPs 'rule'; Law & order; command and control; Lombardi, Patton, McArthur; take charge, delegate and make bulk of decisions; like large teams; like personal touch, not electronic voice mail, e-mail or fax	Collegial; consensual; participation and spirit in workplace is important, as is level playing field; believe management is magic and leadership an art	Egalitarian, not hierarchical; skilled at supporting and developing quality teams; skilled at changing directions, projects "on a dime;" promote involvement, participation; leadership is a job; fair; competent; straight forward, technological communication is strong	Likes to work with bright, creative people; appreciates heroics; wants to have a large impact on work and the work place; newest hardware and technology motivates

6. REINVENTING IDENTITY

"It's all right letting yourself go as long as you can let yourself back."
— Mick Jagger

Learning Objectives:

1. Explore the dilemmas retirees face which lead to rediscovering self without work/title
2. Discuss the application of the Johari Window model to assist clients in expressing authenticity and engaging in self-discovery
3. Understand the importance of sense of purpose/meaning/contribution in retirement, and how to replace recognition and achievement
4. Discover the magic of living in the moment (not regretting past or anticipating future) and its benefits to retirees

Review of Chapter 5:

1. How can you help your clients decide whether or not to continue working in retirement?

2. What are three of the kinds of work options retired clients should consider?

3. How can we help our clients counter age discrimination?

4. What are some of the challenges that arise when Traditionals and Baby Boomers work together?

Existential Questions Emerge Again

Early in life, most people consider such questions as "Who (or what) is God?" "Why am I here?" and "What is the meaning of life?" But the answers we find to those questions in childhood, in our teens, and in our early adulthood may need to be re-examined in retirement. And some people never ponder these questions until they retire!

Finding meaning once one's job has ended and title has gone away can be very difficult for clients who have had their personal identity closely tied to their work. They may have feelings like "I don't know who I am without my work" or "If I am not productive, my life has no meaning." They may wonder what they will do with themselves if they don't have to work. And some people, after a brief stint of retirement, go back to work simply to avoid the discomfort these questions raise!

So how can we help clients find the "real self" beneath their work identity? Coaching questions and techniques such as the following can be used:

- Ask, "Who is the you that did the work?"
- Close your eyes and just pay attention to your breathing for a moment. "Who is the 'self' that is observing your breathing?"
- Name your 10 best traits that have nothing to do with work.
- Ask your best friends and family what your best features are; and breathe it in!
- Affirm: I have value just because I am.
- Write a list of your defining moments in life. Then, notice how many of them were non-work related and what traits you were demonstrating that didn't require you to prove anything to be worthwhile.
- Give yourself a new title! Examples:
    - Experiencer of life
    - Adventurer
    - Pursuer of truth
    - Laid back Larry
    - Connoisseur of new experiences
- Put your name and new title on "personal cards" (same size as business cards but not used in the traditional way) and pass them out to those with whom you want to share them

In *It's Only Too Late If You Don't Start Now,* Barbara Sher suggests that clients ask these eight questions of themselves in revisiting the "big issues of life":

1. Where am I going?
2. Did I do the right thing with my time so far?
3. What's ahead?
4. What are my greatest fears?
5. What do I really want in my future?
6. What do I definitely not want any more of?
7. What regrets would I hate to have when I look back on my life in later years?
8. Why am I on this planet?

Can you think of other ideas?

NOTES:

Allowing Authenticity

It seems ironic that babies are born into the world as spontaneous, totally real and authentic beings, and then spend the next 30, 40, 50, or more years of their lives learning to conform to society, family, and cultural norms. Of course, some rebel, some never stray far from their true self. But many of us leave parts of our true selves behind in our journey through life.

In her book, *It's Only Too Late If You Don't Start Now,* Barbara Sher suggests:

> *"The truth is, there's somebody inside you who hasn't happened yet, who's been waiting to come on the scene and create a new life. One that was never possible until now."*

And later:

> *"That centered, conscious self you had before you entered your fertile years is the same self that is about to return now that you're leaving them."*

The premise of her book is that retirement is a time of growth, renewal, and the emergence of new parts of ourselves, *not* (as is usually assumed) a time of decline. What if you (and your clients) changed your perspective to expect growth instead of decline? How would it change expectations, assumptions and eventually the actual experience of "retirement"?

Our authentic self is the part of us that is real, genuine, and truly "us." When we are able to be who we feel we really are in our work (if any), with our close family and friends, and in other life activities, psychologists say it releases life energy and reduces the stress that comes from trying to be something we really are not.

The Johari Window is a useful model to help our clients determine how authentic they are in their life already. It is pictured in Figure 13:

Figure 13 - Johari Window

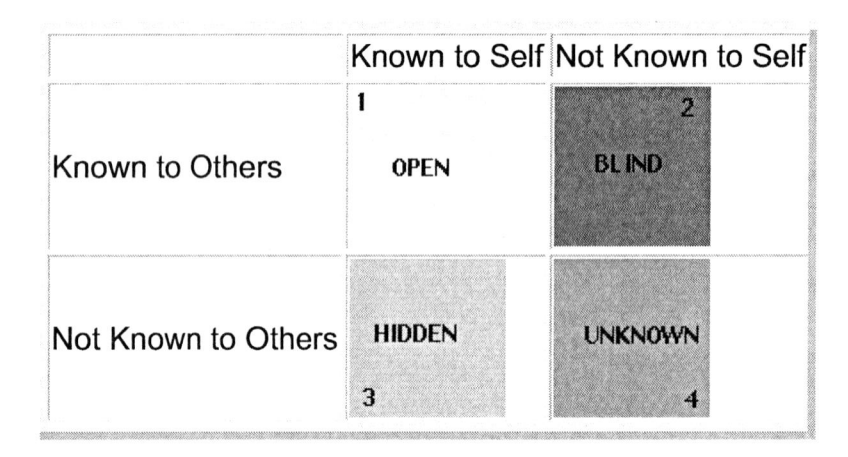

	Known to Self	Not Known to Self
Known to Others	1 OPEN	2 BLIND
Not Known to Others	HIDDEN 3	UNKNOWN 4

The Johari Window was named after its inventors, "Joe" and "Harry" (Joseph Luft and Harry Ingham), and is one of the most useful models describing the process of human interaction. A four paned "window," as illustrated above, divides personal awareness into four different types, as represented by its four quadrants: open, hidden, blind, and unknown. The lines dividing the four panes are like window shades, which can move as an interaction progresses.

1. The "open" quadrant represents things that I know about myself and that you also know about me. Physical characteristics such as the color of one's eyes might be an example here, as well as basic information like address, phone number, etc.

2. The "blind" quadrant is comprised of things that you know about me, but of which I am unaware. We use the term "blind spots" in coaching in the same way: the coach recognizes a pattern or barrier in the client of which the client is unaware, so for the client it is a blind spot. For greatest authenticity, a person would work with a coach, participate in personal growth seminars and workshops, take assessments, and use similar methods to bring more and more of the content of this window to conscious awareness so that it can be consciously accepted or rejected.

3. In the "hidden" quadrant reside things that I know about myself, but you do not know – and that I may not want you to know. Secret information, hidden agendas, things that if disclosed might not make me look good in your eyes, all fall into this quadrant. The more we can open this up to those close to us, and ideally to most of the people with whom we interact, the more authentic we can become.

4. And the final quadrant is the "unknown" -- things that neither I know about myself, nor you know about me. The hidden meaning of a dream, childhood events that have been repressed (such as sexual abuse), and other information or experiences that are truly hidden from both self and others. These may emerge in unexpected ways, such as while watching a movie or listening to a certain type of music – or as

the result of a chance remark someone makes. Embracing both the known and the unknown within ourselves is a doorway through which authenticity often emerges.

How could you use the Johari Window with your clients?

Life Purpose Revisited

> "Life's purpose can be simply defined as a calling, a mission, or an overall theme for your life that transcends your daily activities. It is the quality you have come to earth to develop, the type of service you are here to render, the segment of the planet you have come to enhance or improve or heal. It is much broader than one job or career; it pervades your entire life."
>
> --Marcia Bench, aka Perkins-Reed,
> *When 9 to 5 Isn't Enough*

> "Purpose is the conscious choice of what, where, and how to make a positive contribution to our world. It is the theme, quality, or passion we choose to center our lives around."
>
> --Richard Lieder, *The Power of Purpose*

As you know, the first element of Authentic Retirement is life purpose. This is perhaps the signature trait of the Authentic Retirement model. The author has been advocating the importance of life purpose in career decisions since the mid 1980's, but it was not until the advent of coaching as a profession that life purpose took the central role it deserves. Now, life purpose is something nearly every coach claims to explore when one discusses the issue among coaching colleagues. By discovering and beginning to fulfill their life purpose, clients will finally feel the fulfillment that has eluded them to date.

Definitions of Life Purpose

What is encompassed by the term "life purpose"? First, in a broad sense, we all have a shared overall purpose, in that we are here to discover as much of our true self as we can and to express our true self through our lives to the greatest possible extent. We do this through all of the experiences we have, the people we relate to, the jobs we choose, and the teachers whose message rings true with us.

But that is not our primary emphasis here. Each of us also has a specific life purpose. It is a calling, a mission, or an overall theme for your life that transcends one's daily activities. It is the quality one has come to earth to develop, the type of service the person has been born to render, the way they can enhance or improve some segment of the planet. It is much broader than one job or career; it pervades one's entire life.

If your clients have not adequately clarified their life purpose, or somehow feel that success and fulfillment have eluded them, you may want to share with them a very important principle: People will tend to experience fulfillment in their life to the extent that they are clear about their life purpose.

Qualities of Life Purpose

Fulfilling one's life purpose is fun, joyful, and playful. When we are carrying out our life purpose, we find that the time goes by unnoticed. Hours pass in pure bliss. As a central theme for our life, our life purpose also helps us decide whether to accept a particular job, whether or not to volunteer for a particular cause, and which kinds of relationships -- professional and personal -- will best contribute to fulfilling our purpose.

Why It's Important

When one's life purpose is discovered and expressed, it provides a reason for being, a sense of "coming home," a quality one brings to everyday life, and a motivation for one's activities. Not only is life incomplete without it; there is something missing in the world if each of us does not contribute the gifts they have. Consider these quotes:

> "This is the true joy in life, the being used for a purpose recognized by yourself as a mighty one; the being thoroughly worn out before you are thrown on the scrap heap; the being a force of Nature instead of a feverish selfish little clod of ailments and grievances complaining that the world will not devote itself to making you happy."
>
> --George Bernard Shaw

> "The gifts of each of us and the value of serving others provide our mission in life."
>
> --Richard Bolles, author of *What Color is Your Parachute?*

In the affluent society of the Western world, it may seem that life purpose would be unimportant. However, research tells us otherwise:

"When 60 college students who had attempted suicide were recently surveyed, and 85% of them said the reason was that "life seemed meaningless." 93% of them lacked a sense of purpose in their lives despite socially active lives, academic achievements, and supportive families.

"This happens in the midst of affluent societies and in the midst of welfare states! For too long we have been dreaming a dream from which we are now waking up: the dream that if you just improve the socio-economic status of people, everything will be OK, people will become happy. The truth is that as the struggle for survival has subsided, the question has emerged: survival for what? Ever more people today have the means to live, but no meaning to live for."

--Viktor Frankl, author of
Man's Search for Meaning

And life purpose is particularly critical for retirees to explore. Psychologist Dr. Carl Jung found that if one does not discover one's life purpose and a sense of spirituality by midlife (or beyond), one will never fully develop personally.

NOTES:

Clues to Life Purpose

The 10 clues in Figure 14 which follows are used in Authentic Retirement Worksheet 1 on page 143 to help clients in the life purpose discovery process. They ask clients to look at their life and work from several different perspectives, as though examining a precious stone (or diamond in the rough) from many angles. Then, with a coach's guidance, they uncover the themes that emerge and, ultimately, formulate a statement of their life purpose.

Figure 14 – 10 Clues to Discovering Your Life's Purpose

	10 Clues to Discovering Your Life's Purpose
1	What do you love to do, whether in your spare time or at work?
2	What parts of your present job or life activities do you thoroughly enjoy?
3	What do you naturally do well?
4	What are your ten greatest successes to date (in your eyes)?
5	Is there a cause about which you feel passionate?
6	What are the ten most important lessons you have learned in your life?
7	Are there some issues or perceived problems that have occurred over and over again?
8	What do you daydream about doing?
9	Imagine you are writing your epitaph. What things do you want to be remembered for at the end of your life?
10	What would you do if you knew you could not fail?

Taking the answers to the 10 clues, the next step is to notice any themes in the answers, e.g., do many of them relate to being with people in a particular way, or to solving problems or working with your hands?

Three other processes that may assist the client in discovering their purpose include:

Listen to your intuition. It is often from the intuition that the hints and key aspects of one's purpose emerge. If clients are not accustomed to listening to their intuition, the tips and processes in *Practical Intuition* by Laura Day may be helpful. The intuition is a window into the most authentic parts of people, as well as to their higher purpose in life. Whether it is experienced as an audible voice, a physical sensation or just an urge to call someone, buy a particular book, or attend an event we might not otherwise attend, when they follow it, the meaning behind the sensation eventually becomes clear.

Decide that you matter, and that you can have clarity about your purpose.

> "A sense of purpose is rarely handed to us. We get it by deciding to have it. We get it by deciding that, yes, I matter. A sense of purpose comes from within, and only we know if we have it."
> --Richard Lieder, *The Power of Purpose*

No matter how much you, the coach, believe clients can have clarity about their life purpose, they will not uncover it until they too believe it is possible for them.

Perhaps they are facing one of the obstacles we will discuss in the next section. Or maybe their self-esteem is so low that they need coaching to raise it before they can meaningfully participate in an exploration of their life purpose.

Discover solitude and meditation. It is only through getting quiet that people can hear the answers to the questions life is asking them at these critical junctures such as the retirement transition. Otherwise, the busyness of daily life crowds out the still, small voice that can provide the answers.

One exercise that is simple but powerful is to ask clients to dedicate 15 minutes each morning to just sitting quietly, looking at something beautiful (e.g., scenery out their window) and concentrate on just being there. This is not the time to consciously vision, to solve problems, or to dwell on what isn't working. Rather, it's a time to develop a sense of comfort with oneself, the self that is behind the "doer," that "more of them" that exists apart from their professional or family roles.

Obstacles to Discovering Life Purpose

If discovering one's purpose were easy, everyone would have already done it. Even the 10 clues to life purpose will not result in instant awareness for every client. It is important to be patient with the process and allow it to unfold. On the other hand, clients are often anxious to gain clarity so that they can move on with their retirement planning. One thing that I have discovered is that where it used to take weeks to guide clients to their life purpose, by adding the QuantumShift!™ coaching techniques you will learn in the QuantumShift! Coaching course (the second course required for certification as a Certified Professional Retirement Coach) to the process, clients can usually articulate their purpose statement within a couple of coaching sessions.

There are at least four common obstacles which may arise when clients are experiencing difficulty clarifying their purpose:

1. **Overlooking the value of an interest, skill or passion by assuming that everyone has it.** Certainly, we all have natural strengths and gifts. And we often tend to overlook the very things that people have always told us we're good at doing, or that have always been our "role" or "duty" when our family or close friends plan an activity. This obstacle requires the objective feedback of a third party (e.g., a coach) to help clients see their specialness.

2. **Insisting that one's life purpose be completely unique and different from anyone else's.** Many of the activities and goals represented by a purpose statement are far too large for one person to accomplish, and are outside of their own individual circle of influence. So for more than one person to be committed to that same purpose – or a similar one -- will simply accelerate the transformation process in the world – or the segment in which clients wish to contribute.

3. **Feeling the pressures of just needing to make a living.** This is a common trap for people in their non-working years, in pre-retirement. But once one retires, the door can finally open to explore this important topic!

4. **Thinking that only "special people" have a life purpose, and our clients are not special people.** The truth is, everyone has a purpose, not just writers, artists, musicians or religious leaders (or insert the category of your choice). Discovering it inevitably increases one's life satisfaction. However, some people do not feel the longing to explore it until later in life; others begin early.

NOTES:

Examples of Purpose Statements

The life purpose statement itself -- if it is to be useful as the central theme of one's life -- should be articulated in a specific format, divided into two parts: the *essence*, which is relatively unchanged over one's life, and the *expression*, which changes as life circumstances change. Following are some examples of the essence portion – the hardest for most people to articulate – of several life purpose statements:

- To increase the harmony and love in the world through…
- To be a positive influence on women and children through…
- To help working mothers achieve the balance they desire through…
- To help people communicate with themselves and others as honestly and courageously as possible through…
- To promote win-win conflict resolution and increase world peace through…
- To find my own path and help others find their path through…
- To provide environments where self-healing can occur through…
- To help people discover their purpose and express their calling while they're still alive through…

As people mature, they may refine the way they state the essence portion, but the fundamental theme can be traced from cradle to grave. It is expressed through childhood relationships, college education, early careers, starting a family, releasing children to move out on their own, retirement, and beyond. These latter circumstances are the changing expression portion which evolves as our life unfolds.

A sample life purpose statement including both parts might read:

> *"My life purpose is to increase the harmony and love in the world through volunteering in the local Big Brother/Big Sister program, using a harmonious communication approach in my relationships, pursuing peace in all of my personal and professional relationships, maintaining my personal mental and physical health, being involved in my church, and teaching my grandchildren to seek harmony instead of discord."*

Implementing Life Purpose

Even as clients begin to explore the other elements of their Authentic Retirement, they can begin to live a more purpose-centered life by implementing their life purpose, as they understand it. Here are several easy ways to do this.

1. **Do the activities related to your life purpose first thing in the morning.** This will allow you to do what is important to you before other distractions have a chance to tempt you off course.

2. **Whenever you have a decision to make, ask which of your options will take you closer to your life purpose.** Usually, one of your options will be more joyful than the other(s). This will be the one that leads to the fulfillment of your life purpose. Each small step builds on the last, and soon you are living the life of your dreams!

3. **Be willing to change.** To fulfill your life purpose, you must be willing to change anything that does not take you there. If you are harboring resistance, fear, or old programming, merely stating to the Universe a willingness to chance it will propel you in the direction you want to go. You may not know the precise steps to take, but your willingness will lead you to take the right action for you.

4. **Think of your life purpose as an organizing principle for your life (see Figure 15 at the end of this chapter).** If you imagine that your life purpose is the "hub" of a wheel, you can continue your efforts to implement it by moving out through the other rings of the wheel. Next, you examine your roles: which of them serve your purpose and which do not? Can you, either gradually or immediately, eliminate the roles that no longer serve your newfound purpose? Then you consider our long-term goals and life vision, both. What do you want to have accomplished in three years? Five years? Over your lifetime? Setting long-term goals that facilitate the expression of your purpose ensures that you will feel fulfilled, not just satisfied that you accomplished another goal, because your purpose is being realized.

For the goals that you wish to accomplish within the next year or so, you then set short-term subgoals articulating the "goals within the goals" that you want to achieve, then the specific actions you will take to do so. And finally, you use principles of smart time and stress management to daily execute the steps toward your goals. Thus your life purpose becomes an "organizing principle" for the rest of your life and the basis for a career and life plan. Let's use Sally, a woman approaching retirement, as an example of how this process can work.

Example:

Life purpose statement: To help people communicate better and leave a legacy through consulting with family-owned businesses, conscious relationships with my partner and children, volunteering at nonprofit organizations, and building my self-esteem through assertiveness training, physical fitness, and investing toward my retirement.

Role evaluation: current roles include CFO for hotel business, budding entrepreneur (family business consultant), friend, investor, docent at local museum, spiritual seeker, yoga practitioner, lover; desire to phase out of CFO role and expand entrepreneur role with other roles remaining a total of 25% of total

Long-term goal: To become an internationally known speaker in the field of family business

Short-term subgoals:

- Improve speaking skills
- Become visible within local and, eventually, national hotel and family business associations
- Learn how to price and promote speaking services

Action plans:

- Join Toastmasters to improve speaking skills
- Present proposal to speak at regional hotel association conference
- Join National Speakers Association and network with other established professional speakers re: pricing and promotion

Time/stress management: Drawing from assortment of scheduling, organization, relaxation, and other skills, manage time and stress appropriately to execute plan and achieve goals

Figure 15: Life Purpose as an Organizing Principle

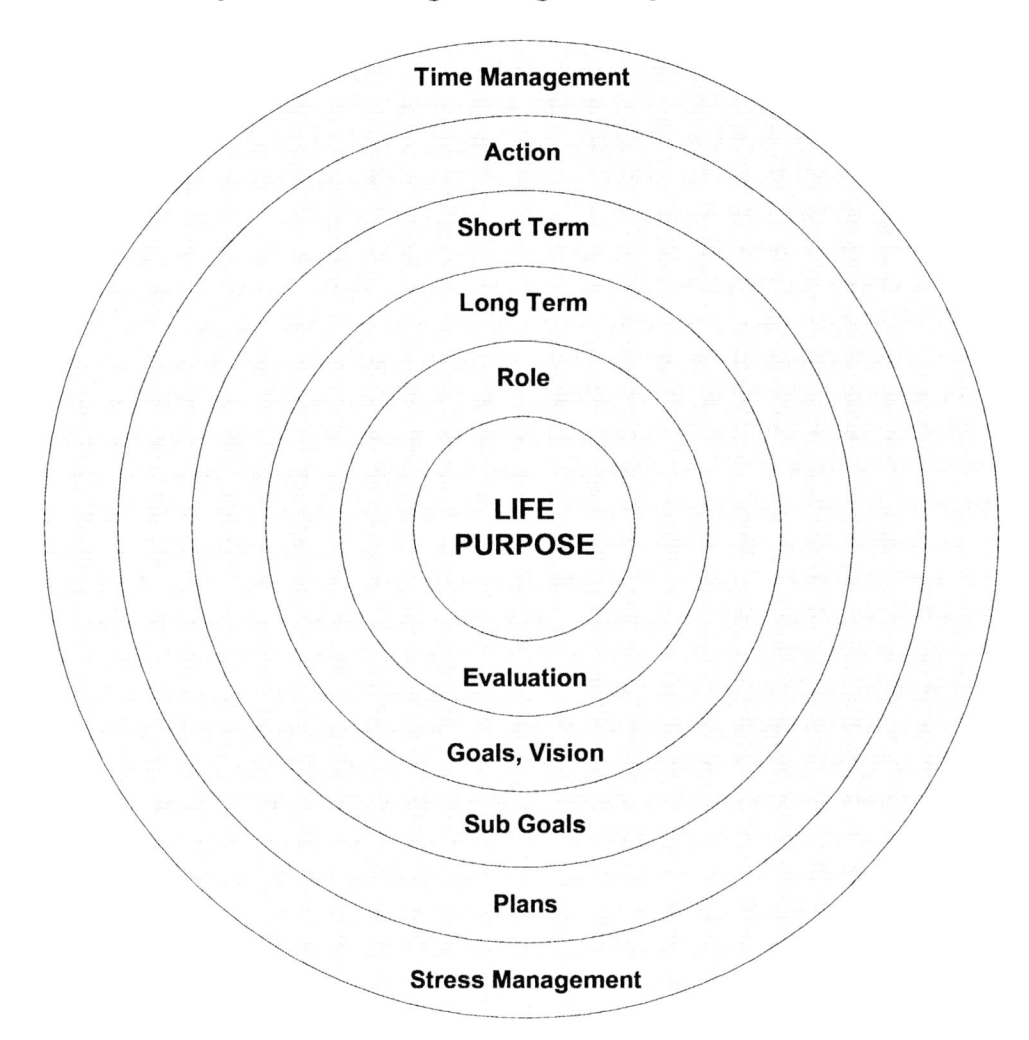

Concentric circles labeled from center outward:
- LIFE PURPOSE
- Role
- Long Term
- Short Term
- Action
- Time Management

And from center outward (bottom):
- Evaluation
- Goals, Vision
- Sub Goals
- Plans
- Stress Management

Reprinted from *Thriving in Transition* by Marcia Bench

NOTES:

Living in the Moment

One of the ICF Core Coaching Competencies is to learn to "dance in the moment" (ICF Core Coaching Competencies 4a: "Is present and flexible during the coaching process, dancing in the moment.") Just as we need to learn this as coaches, our clients need to learn – or relearn! – the same principle in retirement. It is never too late to start!

Clients who tend to worry about the future (e.g., running out of money or losing good health), or who seem fixated on the past can benefit from focusing on development of this skill. Following are some practices that can help clients learn a present-moment focus:

- *Meditation:* any technique that helps clients focus on one thing, such as their breath, a candle flame, or an idea/mantra (e.g., breathe in love, breathe out fear), done on a daily basis, develops focus. As other thoughts enter one's mind, just imagining them as clouds floating by and allowing them to pass as one gently returns to the object of focus is suggested.
- *Avoiding multitasking.* Recent studies have shown that people who multi-task (do more than one thing at once) only achieve 40 percent productivity at each task. So it's actually self-defeating! By consciously choosing the next activity, and concentrating on seeing it through to completion, they not only become more effective at what they are doing; they avoid distractions and can enjoy each moment more.
- *Being adaptable.* Just as a surfer rides the waves, clients must learn to respond and go with the waves of their lives. Whether it is a moment of ecstasy or tragedy, accepting the experience and choosing their response (as the Thriver described in chapter 4 would do) improves their quality of life and minimizes the stress caused by agonizing over what they will do.

NOTES:

KEY CONCEPTS LEARNED:

7. HEALTH AND AGING

"Of all the self-fulfilling prophecies in our culture, the assumption that aging means decline and poor health is probably the deadliest."
– Marilyn Ferguson, *The Aquarian Conspiracy*

Learning Objectives:

1. Explore the new levels of health that today's retirees can experience
2. Consider the opportunities and challenges in extended life expectancy
3. Increase understanding of myths and fears about aging
4. Examine health care and insurance issues clients may need to consider
5. Learn how to help clients deal with health challenges

Review of Chapter 5:

1. How can we assist clients who struggle with who they are after they no longer have a work title?

2. What is the Johari Window?

3. What are four common obstacles to discovering one's life purpose?

New Vistas of Health

Average life expectancy has increased substantially in recent years, due in part to medical advances and in part – some would say – to evolution. Those born in 1945 can expect to live to age 61.4, and for those born in 1965 (the end of the Baby Boom), life expectancy is over 70 years. (Goldberg, Beverly, *Age Works*) Once one reaches age 65, an additional 20 years of life can typically be expected.

In addition, there is an unprecedented number of people over 65 in the U.S. today – and it is expected to continue to accelerate over the coming years. In 1935, only 6.5 Americans were over age 65. By the early 1960's, that number had reached 17 million. Since then it has doubled, and there are now five times as many older adults as there were upon the creation of Social Security in the 1930's, and three times as many as in 1900. As Mark Freedman points out in *Prime Time,* "Half of all the people who have *ever* lived to age 65 are *currently* alive."

But it's not just the sheer numbers, staggering though they are, that are noteworthy. What it means to be 55 or 65 has changed – physically, vocationally, mentally, emotionally and in lifestyle. Through the phenomenon called "downaging," discussed in *Prime Time,* today's 65-year-olds are comparable in vigor and well-being to 45-year-olds in the prior generation, and the trend continues into later ages. The level of health is generally greater (see section on health insurance below), people expect to live longer (and many do), and therefore how people think about their age and station in life is radically different.

Some retiring clients may have been "lucky" up to now in their lives and been able to stay relatively healthy without regular exercise or particularly watching their diet. But with the number of Americans overweight approaching two-thirds and only approximately 15 percent of the population engaged in regular exercise, fewer and fewer people will be able to avoid paying attention to their health. In this area, as with all other areas of retirement planning, there is an element of choice. The retiring client can ask him/herself: *What level of health would I like to experience in my retirement years?* While some diseases and unforeseeable accidents are unavoidable, there is a substantial portion of people's health that *is* a result of personal choice.

Ten years of research done by John Rowe, M.D. and Robert Kahn, Ph.D., both members of the MacArthur Foundation Research Network, is outlined in the book *Successful Aging.* The authors thoroughly debunk the myth that aging has to be a painful process of debilitation. Their research has shown that the influence of genetics shrinks proportionately as one gets older, while social and physical habits become increasingly integral to one's state of health, both mental and physical. Some surprising results are that an inactive person is worse off health-wise than a smoker who exercises regularly. And lifestyle and attitude outweigh genes in determining level of health in later years.

To make and sustain change of any kind usually requires a vision of what the person wants or desires, and then accessing the motivation to achieve it – that is, the benefits of reaching the goal or experiencing the desired state. To that end, you can use the questionnaire, "My Retirement Health," Tool 16 in the Retirement Coaches Toolbox (page 174), here.

A few of the secrets of a healthier life include:

- Eat a balanced diet with at least five servings of fresh fruits and vegetables daily and minimal fast food, sugar and starches
- Exercise nearly every day
- Avoid drugs, tobacco, and excess alcohol
- Get adequate sleep

- Cultivate a positive attitude
- Keep mentally as well as physically fit
- Have several close friends
- Spend time in nature

Are there others you believe are also critical?

NOTES:

Longer Life: Challenge or Opportunity?

Perhaps you have heard the saying, "Whether you think you can or think you cannot, you are right." The same principle applies to aging: whether you think it is good or think it is bad, you're right! While we cannot change our clients' physical health or their past, we can help them change how they think about the remainder of their life. Is it a challenge, fraught with hard times, illness and decline? Or is it an opportunity for growth and development of new aspects of themselves – including new levels of health?

Part of the challenge with retirement – if clients have not already confronted it in midlife – is that it forces people to realize they are mortal, and that they will not live forever. Many people postpone writing their will because they do not want to face their own demise! But there can be an advantage in facing one's mortality: it stimulates a commitment to fully living one's life now! Here is a coaching question suggested by Barbara Sher that can get our clients thinking about the possibilities: *"How do you live now that you know you will not live forever?"* The sky is the limit! How big can you and your clients dream?

Jenny Joseph, in her poem "When I am an old woman, I shall wear purple," captures the essence of both fun in aging and authenticity:

> *When I am an old woman, I shall wear purple*
> *with a red hat that doesn't go, and doesn't suit me.*
> *And I shall spend my pension on brandy and summer gloves*
> *and satin candles, and say we've no money for butter.*
> *I shall sit down on the pavement when I am tired*
> *and gobble up samples in shops and press alarm bells*
> *and run my stick along the public railings*
> *and make up for the sobriety of my youth.*

*I shall go out in my slippers in the rain
and pick the flowers in other people's gardens
and learn to spit.*

*You can wear terrible shirts and grow more fat
and eat three pounds of sausages at a go
or only bread and pickles for a week
and hoard pens and pencils and beer nuts and things in boxes.*

*But now we must have clothes that keep us dry
and pay our rent and not swear in the street
and set a good example for the children.
We must have friends to dinner and read the papers.
But maybe I ought to practice a little now?
So people who know me are not too shocked and surprised
When suddenly I am old, and start to wear purple.*

Consider these questions for your clients who are struggling to see the positive side of aging:

- If you knew you had 30 more years to live, how would you live them differently than the years you've already lived?
- What can you do now, as a retired person, that you couldn't do when you were working and raising your family?
- Think of someone you know that seems unruffled – and even delighted! – by their aging process. Interview them and find out how they do it.
- What could your mantra be for the "new you" that is yet to be?

What gets in the way of our clients' seeing the positive side of life?

Is optimism learned, or are we born with it?

NOTES:

Myths and Fears About Aging

Many of the common stereotypes and expectations people have about aging are rooted in the age of the "old model of retirement" and are no longer valid. Whatever the assumptions your clients may have about age and aging, we can encourage them to revisit them, challenge them, and consciously choose what they wish to experience as the years unfold. What are some of the myths you have heard about aging? Write them below:

A few to consider:

- All old people are pretty much the same (when in fact personalities as well as approach to retirement and aging vary widely)
- Old dogs can't learn new tricks (in fact one of the secrets of good health as we age is continually challenging our minds with new experiences)
- Old people are isolated and lonely (have you visited a retirement community lately? Many retirees are more active than their children in a variety of hobbies, classes, and activities!)
- Older people can't do all the things younger people can (see below)
- It is too late to learn a new hobby or go back to school (on the contrary, learning keeps people young)
- If I have not realized my dreams yet, I never will (now may be just the time!)
- Once I turn 65 (or any specific age) it's downhill from there! (as discussed earlier, it can be a time of growth, not decline)

Consider this recent headline, which counters myths about athletic competition:

"America's Top Senior Athletes Redefine Aging at The 1999 National Senior Games - The Senior Olympics Gold Rush Begins... "

The story http://www.go60.com/myths.htm went on to say that with a record number of entrants, the 1999 National Senior Games constitute the largest athletic competition in the world. Registered athletes range from Baby Boomers to World War II veterans. Twenty-five percent of the participants were in their 50s; 43 percent were in their 60s; 26 percent were in their 70s; and .4 percent are in their 90s. All 50 states were represented, with Florida sending the largest number of registrants (730). Maryland, Texas and California sent delegations of 599, 576 and 562 athletes, respectively.

Barbara Sher treats the topic of aging humorously and well in her book, *It's Only Too Late If You Don't Start Now*. She challenges even the notion that we define ourselves by our age, since each individual's experiences are unique, and many retirees have had their greatest successes in retirement (e.g., Colonel Sanders, Grandma Moses). Sher suggests four rules to handle aging:

1. Don't decide you're too old to do something before you really are.
2. Time is clay. Make something.
3. If you've got a big dream, go for it. But never believe it's your last.
4. Watch out for premature regrets. (There's a good chance it hasn't started yet!)

NOTES:

Health Care and Insurance

The aging of the Boomers is also affecting company benefits for the workforce. The number of workers between ages 55 and 69 is projected to grow 31 million from 1995 to 2020, and is already beginning to create a crisis in health care coverage and costs. Perhaps the best recent summary of data on health care and medical benefits is that of the Employee Business Research Institute at http://www.ebri.org/findings/health_fndings.htm (June 2004). Highlights include:

- In 2002, 12.9 percent of individuals aged 55 to 64 were without health insurance, a slight change from 1994, when 12.8 percent were uninsured.
- Adults ages 55 to 64 are the least likely group of adults to be without health insurance.
- Among workers ages 55 to 64, 78.5 percent had employment-based coverage, compared with 55.1 percent of retirees ages 55 to 64.
- Workers in the service sector are much less likely to have employment-based health benefits than workers in manufacturing. Studies have found that the movement of workers from the manufacturing sector to the service sector accounts for approximately 10 to 15 percent of the decline in employment-based health insurance coverage.

There have been concerns that increased longevity, resulting from greater life expectancy, could crush the health care system. However, according to the National Bureau of Economic Research Program Report on the Economics of Aging (http://www.nber.org/aging.html), "While population aging has created additional health and long-term care needs, the potential cost has been moderated – at least in the short run – by a significant long-term decline over time in the functional limitations of older people." So people are living longer but staying healthier, ameliorating the projected financial impact on health care by the aging Boomers.

That does not mean, however, that health insurance premiums are staying the same! A survey of 435 private-sector firms with 1000 or more workers that currently offer health benefits to retirees found that more than half of the companies planned to raise premiums and increase co-payments in the coming three years, and nearly a quarter planned to eliminate health coverage for future retirees. (See "Retirees Face Increased Premiums," by Janelle Carter, Associated Press 2002 in Resource List). And 82 percent planned to increase retiree premiums over the next three years as well as increase prescription drug co-payments. With private health insurance costs increasing at the rate of more than 12 percent per year, many pre-retirees may find themselves faced with a rude awakening if they have failed to budget for private health insurance once they retire.

What is the lesson for us as retirement coaches?

When Health Issues Arise

Most people, sooner or later, face a health issue. Whether it is injuries from an automobile accident, cancer, a heart attack, or other ailments, learning how best to get through them can make the significant difference in both current and future quality of life.

The author experienced cancer a couple of years ago, and through months of treatment, developed several strategies that were very helpful and which may benefit your retiree clients facing similar issues:

1. Become as informed as you can about your condition. It is amazing how many people continue to take a passive role in their health care. The old model said that the doctors were the possessors of all knowledge when it came to health, and that we should listen to them and do everything they said without questioning. That was then; this is now! Today, with extensive medical information readily available to the lay person on the Internet, and hundreds of books on every imaginable condition available at the local bookstore, consumers have become much more informed and sophisticated. Encourage your clients to read what they can about their diagnosis, to talk to others who have had the condition, get involved on bulletin boards and information sharing groups (see below) and otherwise learn both about the condition and the treatment options. Then, when meeting with their physician(s), they can ask informed questions and better decide the course of action to take.

2. Get more than one opinion. It is common for doctors to differ in both diagnosis and recommended treatment of various conditions. Particularly when it is something as major as cancer or heart disease, suggest that clients take their test results to another specialist in that field for a consultation to obtain their medical opinion. If the two doctors agree, chances are increased that the course of treatment is correct. If they disagree, a third opinion may need to be sought to gain consensus. And whether talking to one's primary physician, a specialist, or a second opinion provider, it is good practice to take another person along to the appointment or tape record what is said. As a clever advertisement currently running reads, "Most people suffer a 60 percent hearing loss when sitting in their doctor's examining room."

3. Seek support – and keep people informed of your progress. One of the Thriver Traits, you may recall, is a healthy support system. Hopefully your client will have already established relationships with such people before he/she becomes ill. But even if they have not, identifying and becoming involved in existing support groups (locally or on the Internet) of people with similar health conditions can provide encouragement, information, and a forum to ask the questions that are hard to ask. It can be very helpful to establish a chat group on Yahoogroups http://groups.yahoo.com, which is a free service allowing people with a common interest to exchange email among the group around their common interest. In this case, the common interest is the patient! Each week clients can provide an update on their progress, and receive wonderful supportive messages from their group of caring friends and family. Knowing others care about you goes a long ways! In addition, if the client needs someone to help with house cleaning, grocery shopping, or similar tasks, a support team can be organized for this purpose.

4. Plan personal rewards or fun activities as benchmarks to look forward to. During medical treatment or healing from surgery, it helps to have something to anticipate. Perhaps each month during an illness clients plan a trip out of town, walks in the forest, visits to the beach, and the like. The extent to which this is possible will depend on how physically restricted the patient/client is by his/her illness. And of course physician's orders must be observed.

5. Keep a positive attitude and visualize health. Our attitude toward any life experience determines largely whether we will overcome it or it will overcome us. It may need to be bolstered during health challenges! Perhaps the visualization tapes of Dr. Carl Simonton for cancer, or relaxation tapes, recorded affirmations, or flowers in the room every day will help maintain a positive attitude when it is difficult to do so. Rather than thinking "Why me?" and feeling sorry for oneself, clients can simply affirm that the experience has come for a reason, and that while they may not understand it now, they trust that the process of healing is happening.

6. Find an outlet for difficult feelings. No matter how well people may do keeping a positive outlook, there is still the shock of the diagnosis, the helpless feeling when faced with the worst case scenario, and even rage that this has happened to them. Each person facing such emotions must find an outlet for them. Talking to one's spouse or friends or support group can help, as can journaling. Psychologist Dr. James Pennebaker found, in a research study, that journaling about one's feelings when going through any transition will shorten its duration and make it more tolerable. When journaling and conversations with friends are inadequate, consulting a therapist or social worker may be appropriate.

NOTES:

Case Study

Jacqueline retired two years ago at age 58 from a career as a manager in an aerospace firm. Her employer, Aerospace Inc., provided health insurance for retirees and a generous severance package when she retired. Married to a retired dentist, Don, Jacqueline has been feeling very "old" lately. Though they went on a two-week trip to Mexico when she retired, they have not left home since. She has been feeling more aches and pains lately, and is convinced she has a chronic illness. Aerospace Inc. just informed her that they would be terminating her retirement health coverage in 6 months. Don's only coverage is through Medicare, since he is over 65, and she doesn't know how she will pay for health insurance if her employer doesn't provide it.

When she was young, Jacqueline used to dream of playing the guitar, but she never took lessons and believes now it is too late to begin. She doesn't really have any hobbies, though she gets together with a group of 4 other ladies that retired with her from Aerospace Inc. once a week for lunch.

She has come to you for retirement coaching because her life seems boring and "blah."

Where would you start if you were to work with Jacqueline?

What would her primary coaching issues be as they relate to health and aging?

KEY CONCEPTS LEARNED:

8. SOCIAL/RELATIONSHIP SHIFTS

"Marriage is a great institution, but I'm not ready for an institution yet."
– Mae West

Learning Objectives:

1. Explore the top five areas that impact couples that are preparing for or going through the transition of retirement
2. Consider timing issues when not both partners retire at the same time
3. Understand the importance of a network of friends outside of work
4. Examine new family dynamics such as the "sandwich generation" and grandparents raising their grandchildren

Review of Chapter 7:

1. How is today's retirees' experience of health different from those in prior generations?

2. What can we do to coach someone who considers their retirement years to be a time of decline?

3. What are some myths of aging clients need to challenge?

4. How can we help clients who are going through a health challenge?

Impact of Retirement on Couples

The old retiree stereotype held that at age 65, the husband would retire and the wife would be at home, they would travel, work in the yard, play golf, volunteer, spend time with family, etc. That has now changed. Multiple scenarios can now be expected. In a minority of cases, the old stereotype may still occur. But as more and more women have worked outside the home and will be planning their own retirement, many couples will face (and have to adjust to) two retirements, one by each spouse. Second, as companies consolidate to be more "lean and mean," some workers are presented with early retirement packages. Their retirement date can be substantially accelerated if a generous package is presented. And a third scenario is that one spouse continues to work, and the other retires first. If both partners are not prepared emotionally and financially for these scenarios (and others they may encounter), the transition is more difficult.

The Cornell Study (see Resource List) faced this issue head on:

> *"The transition to retirement is particularly stressful, especially when one spouse retires before the other," says the study. "During this time, couples fight much more and are significantly less satisfied with their marriages. Once both spouses are settled into retirement from their careers, however, marital satisfaction rebounds and couples report the highest levels of marital satisfaction with the least conflict, compared with their peers.*
>
> *" 'It's not being retired but becoming retired that seems most stressful for marriages,' "* said Phyllis Moen, a professor of sociology and human development at Cornell.
>
> *"Newly retired men and women both report more marital conflict than either their not-yet retired or long-term retired (more than two years) counterparts. Marital quality slumps the most among couples in which only one spouse retires, especially when the husband retires and the wife keeps working.*
>
> *"When women first retire, however, they go through a spell of low marital satisfaction, whether their husbands are working or not. But they become more satisfied if they either go back to work in other jobs or their husbands retire and then go back to work. Women, especially employed women, report more marital conflicts when their husbands retire and do not go back to work.*
>
> *" 'Men, however, show a different pattern. They reported the highest marital conflict if they retire but their wives haven't yet. When both husbands and wives move into retirement more or less together, men become much happier with their marriages,' "* said Moen."

How would you coach a man who is struggling with marital discord as he approaches retirement?

What about a woman who has just retired and facing the "low marital satisfaction" described in the study? Would coaching or counseling be most appropriate? How do you know?

Top Five Areas That Affect A Couple's Relationship Retirement Transition When One or Both Retire

There are five primary areas of a couple's relationship that are impacted by the impact of one or both partners. They are: (1) income and taxes, (2) maintaining communication, (3) compromising, (4) role assignments, and (5) gratification.

1. Managing Income and Taxes

The financial area of the retirement process is central to retirement planning. Each person's needs are unique, as is their portfolio (balancing risk and reward) and their income needs and desires. Thus the approach to each individual's financial planning for their retirement years is also unique.

The following article "When Just One of You is Retiring" written by Katy Read for *Reader's Digest* (see Resource List), is a great primer on managing finances, income and taxes.

While chapter 3 addressed finances in general, the *Readers Digest* article addresses issues specifically for couples, such as the impact on the couple's tax rate when one person retires, and the possible counterbalancing factor of beginning to withdraw from one's retirement accounts.

For more articles on pre-retirement and post retirement, including financial planning, see the research section of the Society of Actuaries web site here: http://www.soa.org/ccm/content/?categoryID=222005

2. Maintaining Communication

When one spouse works and the other is retired, daily routines change, and schedules are not always intertwined. Maintaining open communication is imperative, both to stay connected to each other's emotional state, and to understand how the other spouse is dealing with the transition.

Gay and Kathlyn Hendricks http://www.hendricks.com, suggest three primary areas of so-called "conscious relationships": feeling, truth, and agreements/responsibility. Taking the quiz at this link: http://survey.hendricks.com/cgi-local/survey.pl?survey=integrity_test can help couples determine the areas in which they are struggling most, and can focus on improving, as they go through the retirement transition.

Consider also the following principles in marital communication that particularly apply during the retirement transition:

1. "Good marriage communication cannot be developed by talking about the weather, or watching soap operas and football on TV"

2. "Sometimes we use up all of our communication skills when we are out in the world, and have little left by the time we come home"

3. "You cannot not communicate"

4. "Traits expected or needed at work can cause a rift in communication if those same traits are carried over to home life."

Source: "Communication: Key to Understanding in Marriage and Family Life" by Herbert L. Lingren (see Resource List).

A couple of potential roadblocks in maintaining communication could be:

1. Different schedules (working spouse works night shift)
2. Work requires spouse to travel, however retired spouse financially cannot travel

3. Retiring spouse wants to travel but working spouse cannot get time off from work
4. One spouse "shuts down" when facing uncomfortable feelings and does not let the other know what he/she is feeling
5. After raising children, wife went back to work and is thriving in a job she loves, and when husband retires and wants to travel, she is unwilling to leave the job she loves

Retirement can also cause long-standing issues between the partners to come to the surface again. And if any of these circumstances continue without the next principle, compromise, the wedge in the relationship can be so great as to lead to divorce.

Since we are coaches and not therapists, it is critical to know when issues between couples are more suitable for a therapist to handle. The guidelines in Tool 17 of the Retirement Coaches Toolbox, "Top Ten Indicators to Refer to a Mental Health Professional" (provided by the ICF), on page 176 can help.

NOTES:

3. Compromising

Merriam-Webster dictionary defines the word *compromise* as:

> *1 a : settlement of differences by arbitration or by consent reached by mutual concessions b : something intermediate between or blending qualities of two different things*

No matter whether a couple is working or retired, living together provides ongoing challenges and opportunities for personal growth for a healthy relationship. During the retirement transition, the give and take of compromise is a must to continue to adjust to changing schedules, lifestyle, and roles of both you and your spouse.

For example:
1. If both are retired, one may want to travel and the other who traveled extensively in their career wants to stay home and work around the yard and do some remodeling inside home.
2. If one spouse works and the other is retired, the working spouse may come home too tired to go out to a friend's home for dinner, which would have

provided the retiree an escape from being at home alone and the opportunity to interact with others.

What coaching techniques would you use here?

4. Role Assignments

Role assignments also change when both individuals retire or if one continues to work and the other retires. They could be out of sync if both cannot agree on their new roles.

Examples may be:
1. Who will pick up the cleaning, grocery shopping and paying the bills while one spouse is still working?
2. Will the wife who is retired begin doing the yard work or taking the car into be serviced? Or the husband beginning to do cooking and housework?

There maybe a point the working spouse becomes jealous of the retiree, having time to do things he/she wants to do, and they still have to get up and go to work every day. Resentment could build after time that the working spouse "escapes" to an interactive, challenging and stimulating work environment each day and they are left alone at home.

What other issues do you see arising from the changing of roles?

Some coaching questions that can help clients work through this change might include:

- What does it mean to you to be a "good wife"/"good husband"?
- Are you willing to consider shifting your role now that you are retired/your spouse is retired?
- Do you want to be right or do you want to be happy?
- What is more important to you: people (and your marriage) or things?
- What are you willing to do to have what you want?

- What is your part in this?
- What are you willing to do to sustain your marriage?

List others below:

5. Gratification

After retirement many retirees miss the gratification and sense of satisfaction that came with their job. As a result, depression -- along with low morale -- can set in if the retiree doesn't have a plan in place to replace work in providing that gratification during their retirement years.

The Cornell Study, cited above, found that post-retirement employment is beneficial to men in this regard, and those who worked in retirement had the highest morale and lowest depression. Those who did not know what to do with their time had low morale and a high proportion of depression.

The work options discussed in chapter 5, applied to each spouse and coordinated with each other, can address the gratification need directly.

NOTES:

Reactions of Family and Friends

Before announcing retirement, retirees also need to consider the reaction of their children and other family members. Widely varied reactions can result! What might some of them be?

Some relatives will be happy for the retiring spouse/couple, some may be jealous (especially of early retirement), and others may feel the "implied contract" of their relationship has been broken (e.g. if you will no longer be living in the same neighborhood as a grown child and available at a moment's notice for babysitting).

When coaching a client prior to retirement, asking a series of questions like those which follow can help them anticipate the reaction of relatives to their decision:

- Who will be affected by your retirement decision? (coworkers, spouse, children, close friends, etc.)
- What will their likely reaction be?
- How will you respond?
- How could you temper the announcement to address their anticipated feelings of (loss/jealousy etc.)?

Whether clients are pre-retirement or already in their retirement, they may face resistance from other close relatives or friends. As a coach, it is one of our roles to help them distinguish between which of the issues/dilemmas presented are actually within their control, and which are not; which are "their" issues and which are the reactions of others to their decision. If a person is co-dependent, he may tend to take on the reactions of others as his responsibility when they are not. Providing feedback and probing what the client believes his part of the situation is and what belongs to someone else can help clients make this distinction.

In *Retire Smart, Retire Happy,* Dr. Nancy Schlossberg also suggests holding an "expectation exchange" for those clients for whom it feels appropriate, in which adult children and their retiring parents sit down and discuss their respective expectations of the relationship now that the parent(s) are retiring.

NOTES:

Weaving the Social Web

During their primary working years, some people naturally seek out and nurture a wide circle of friends, others a few deep intimate acquaintances, and still others put such a focus on work and accumulating their retirement nest egg that they "never find time" to develop social relationships. Friendship is critical to overall well-being, especially to women. In a 2000 study published in *Psychological Review,* researchers discovered that the more friends women had, the longer they lived and that they stayed in better health. http://www.apa.org/monitor/julaug00/stress.html

Further, the article continues, women tend to adopt a "tend and befriend" approach, forming alliances with a social group, when faced with stress rather than the traditional male "fight-or-flight" approach.

The good news is, it's never too late to start building a social network. Whether clients already have a solid group of friends or not, it is important to realize where they are socially as they approach retirement and what additional types of relationship could be added to improve their retirement experience. The worksheet "My Social Network," Tool 18 in the Retirement Coaches Toolbox (page 180), can be used with clients focusing on the relationships part of their retirement planning.

NOTES:

Sandwich Generation

Because of the extended life expectancy for today's retirees, many Boomers are in a situation in which prior retirees rarely found themselves: they can be not only adapting to their own retirement (and their changing marriage and social relationships, work situation, and personal identity), but also caring for ailing parents and possibly raising (or being active in the lives of) their grandchildren. This makes for a complex transition!

To successfully navigate each aspect of it, clients can apply the Dynamic Model of Transition discussed in chapter 4 to each aspect separately and chart their way through it. Gradual or sudden decline of one's parents can have a wide range of ramifications:

- The retiree who may have just gotten settled in his/her ideal retirement location may find themselves having to move "back home" to be close to Mom or Dad
- The retiree and his/her siblings may find themselves having to reach consensus on care options for Mom or Dad – and sibling rivalry often emerges alive and well in these situations!
- If the retiree's parent has not done adequate long-term care insurance, health insurance, or estate planning, the retiree may need to spearhead this effort.
- The retiree and his/her siblings may need to move the parent into assisted living or a nursing home, dispose of the parent's home and/or belongings, and similar very difficult decisions. And since health decline is often gradual, decisions may need to be made several times before the process is through.

A complicating factor is the parent's desire: if he/she wishes to remain at home despite ill health, the children are placed in a challenging situation.
- If insurance does not cover nursing home, home health care or other needed care, the retiree and his/her siblings may need to pay some of the parent's living expenses, thus impacting the retiree's financial situation.

The personal feelings of loss of the parent to look up to, the heartache of the parent not recognizing the child when in the throes of Alzheimer's disease or dementia, and other emotional consequences cannot be neatly packaged and dealt with at a convenient time – they affect the retiree on a daily basis! Coaching clients to brainstorm their options and discuss their experience, and referring them to a therapist (or other specialists in senior care) as appropriate can help clients move through this part of the retirement transition.

Grandparent or Parent?

Two to four million or more retirees with grandchildren are now raising those children as the primary caregiver, according to AARP. And 6.3 percent of U.S. children under 18 live in grandparent-headed households. Here again, the best laid plans for retirement can be changed in a moment by this often unexpected situation, whether it is due to substance abuse or incarceration of a parent or due to divorce or death of a parent (the retiree's child).

For information and resources on raising grandchildren, see
http://www.aarp.org/confacts/programs/grandraising.html

In some cases, grandparents may find themselves prohibited from visiting their grandchildren following an acrimonious divorce of their child and his/her spouse. To have visitation rights reinstated, legal action may be required. The grandparents' rights sites at http://www.grandparentsrights.org/ and http://www.grandtimes.com/visit.html provide some basic principles for clients in this situation.

Guidelines include:

- Don't be too aggressive.
- Don't prematurely file a lawsuit.
- Call the local bar association for a referral to an appropriate attorney.
- Avoid involving the grandchildren in the differences the retiree has with his/her child.
- Remember that grandparent visitation rights are not intended or designed to supersede parental authority.
- And be aware that the law applying to your visitation rights is that of the state where the grandchildren live.

Case Study

John and Mary were college sweethearts, and have been married for 38 years! John is turning 60 this year and Mary will be 58. John is an Executive VP at a large investment firm and Mary has built her catering practice over the last 15 years to 100 clients, which keeps her very busy. Both thoroughly enjoy their work, but their work has involved long hours and a significant focus during their primary working lives. They have enjoyed such luxuries as having a housekeeper and being able to take annual trips abroad. They have two married children and 3 grandchildren, all living within 30 miles of John and Mary.

John had targeted retiring at the age of 62, and was looking forward to the next two years of grooming those that he was mentoring. Mary loves what she does and was targeting 60 to retire, which would have been around the same time that John retired. But then John's company decided to reduce its management staff, and John was one of the EVP's that was given an early severance package. John would like Mary to sell her business and retire with him and travel. Mary just signed a new contract with a client that would commit the catering service for all of the events for the next year. She still has her eye on the age of 60 for her retirement and not before. The housekeeper is leaving the state and just gave two weeks' notice. Since John is going to be retired and they could save some money, Mary doesn't feel that they should hire a new housekeeper. And they just received a call from their son, Dave, that his marriage is in trouble and he does not know whether he will be able to obtain custody of his two daughters if they divorce.

Let's review the 5 areas we discussed above:

1. Finances/Taxes: What questions should John and Mary ask here?

2. Maintaining Communication: What communication issues might arise?

3. Compromise: Are there obvious issues on which they may need to compromise?

4. Role Assignments: How are their roles changing? How would you coach them?

5. Gratification: How can John substitute his work gratification in retirement? Should he?

6. Are there any grandparent/sandwich generation issues to address?

NOTES:

KEY CONCEPTS LEARNED:

9. LEISURE AND TRAVEL; RETIREMENT ASSESSMENTS

"He who would travel happily must travel light."
– Antoine de Saint-Exupery

Learning Objectives:

1. Identify tips and traps in leisure in retirement
2. Develop resources and coaching strategies for clients planning extensive travel during retirement
3. Explore assessments coaches can use with retirement clients

Review of Chapter 8:

1. What are the top five areas that impact couples that are preparing for or going through the transition of retirement?

2. How would you coach a couple when both partners do not retire at the same time?

3. How would you coach a client who has no non-work friends and is within six months of retiring?

4. What can a client do if her child divorces and refuses to allow her to visit her grandchildren?

Leisure in Retirement

In the old paradigm of retirement, leisure was the primary focus for most people. And even today, it is a centerpiece. Mark Freedman points out in *Prime Time* that "In 1995, Americans over age 65 could claim seven more hours of free time a week than their counterparts a decade earlier, and ten hours more than in 1975...Next to sleep (35 percent of time use for those over 65), recreation is the biggest single activity in later life."

A full 70 percent of those surveyed in the Cornell Retirement and Well-Being Study retired "to do other things," which assumedly indicates at least some leisure activities. But it is disturbing to note that older adults also watch more television than any other age group does. Researchers at University Maryland and Penn State found that fully half of seniors' free time is spent watching television (Freedman, *Prime Time*). So could it be that many retirees work hard to get to a place in their lives where work is not required, only to find that they don't know how to fill their time other than by passively watching TV?

The exercise "What Will I Do With My Time?," Tool 19 in the Retirement Coaches Toolbox (page 182), provides clients with an opportunity to benchmark their current activities, and then deliberately outline their desired time allocation. If they desire to spend time in an activity that they need to learn, then taking a class in that sport or activity or hobby becomes part of their retirement planning.

NOTES:

Travel: Adventure or Escape?

Many retirees incorporate travel into their retirement lifestyle, whether a celebration trip upon retirement or several trips abroad every year. Others are simply happy to have time to spend "at home," and have little interest in travel.

If clients do plan to travel, it can be helpful to them if we coach them with open-ended questions (with no "right" answers!) such as:

- What is important to you about traveling at this time?
- What is important about that particular destination?
- What do you expect to gain from the trip(s)? (and if it is something that lies within the client and not in a faraway place, to test those assumptions)
- What would be the destination of your dreams?
- How could you go to that place (even if it seems outside your budget) using creative strategies?

Travel in retirement can be a lifestyle, not a two-week vacation as it is by necessity during one's primary working years. It can be helpful for clients to reflect back on prior vacations and consider which were most enjoyable and why. People have widely varying descriptions of what makes a vacation fun. For some it is that "we crammed a lot of activities into a short time." For others, it's that "we didn't do anything but lay by the pool." Still others may rank a vacation or trip most fun because they got to play all the golf or tennis they wanted, or that they didn't have an agenda and just let their instincts guide them through a previously unknown part of their country. The pace, location, accommodations and activities that are satisfying for our clients can be determined in this way and then applied to retirement travel, leaning the odds in favor of a positive experience.

In *How to Retire Happy, Wild, and Free,* Ernie Zelinski offers the following tips (paraphrased and revised by the author) to enhance the traveling experience:

- Choose your destination wisely and be with people you enjoy.
- Incorporate your life passions into your travel plans
- Don't schedule too much and create a stressful experience
- Plan periods of free time to allow for spontaneity
- When traveling by car, don't rush to your destination
- Be more adventurous than you have before
- Visit the place to which you're considering moving to get some direct experience of it
- Check out local cafes and diners and other neighborhood businesses rather than patronizing only the national chains
- Stay in short-term apartments, exchange homes with someone in your desired location through an online service such as http://www.exchangehomes.com , or stay in a bed and breakfast – you'll meet new people and have a more interesting experience
- Visit a place that has special meaning to you (e.g. where your parents were born)
- Design and write a description of your fantasy vacation, no holds barred; then work toward creating it
- Get off the beaten path and experience new things, places and people
- Find a pub, coffee bar or bistro where the locals gather and find out what the people there are really all about
- What is the one thing you would enjoy doing on your vacation more than anything else? Do it!

It used to be that one needed a travel agent to book any air travel, cruises, and the like. Today, with the advent of the Internet, online travel services that anyone can use, it is relatively simple for retirees to plan their own trips. Some of the better known online services include http://www.expedia.com, http://www.travelocity.com, http://www.priceline.com, http://www.hotels.com, http://www.cruisedirect.com and others.

Some web sites and groups specializes in exotic adventures; some cruises cater to seniors. Clients who want to add meaning and an ecological purpose to their travels can consider http://www.ecotourism.org and similar sites. And single seniors can go to http://www.seniorsmatch.com or http://www.whytravelalone.com, "matchmakers" for those seeking travel companions. Retirees wishing to try out a prospective new career or business (whether it would be full-time or part-time) may want to consider http://www.vocationvacations.com/, which allows people the opportunity to try out a vocation risk-free.

The lesson? Whatever the retirees' wishes when it comes to travel, they can be satisfied at a variety of levels of cost.

RV'ing

Traveling in a recreational vehicle is an increasingly popular way to see the country – or the world! The RV industry generates $12 billion per year, and the sale of luxury-end rigs has grown 120-fold since 1991. Whether clients choose a Class A (bus-style), a Class C (like an oversized camper) or a standard or fifth wheel trailer towed behind a pickup, these homes on wheels allow people to see new areas but have their familiar surroundings within their living space. Clubs consisting of owners of specific brands of RV's, as well as those desiring member services such as camping discounts, road service, monthly magazine, and the like such as Good Sam http://www.goodsamclub.com, are available to provide support to those who travel this way. Just pulling into an RV park can be a social experience – RV'ers are very friendly!

For more information on this way of life/travel, see:

New RV'er
http://www.newrver.com/?OVRAW=rv'ing&OVKEY=rv%20ing&OVMTC=standard

Articles about RV'ing: http://www.newrver.com/articleindex.html

RV America http://www.rvamerica.com/index.cfm?ref=google

RV Travel http://www.rvtravel.com/

NOTES:

Retirement Assessments

Since retirement coaching is such a new field, there are relatively few assessment tools directly related to planning the non-financial aspects of retirement. So we are providing you with our own proprietary tools: the Authentic Retirement Worksheets, Retirement Readiness Wheel, and other tools in the Retirement Coaches Toolbox. These tools will be available, along with a guided narrative, in workbook format soon for you to use with your clients.

In this section, we provide a review of other retirement assessments (of the non-financial aspects of the process) that are available at this writing and which you may also want to utilize.

1. Retirement Options. The author of The New Retirement, Dr. Richard Johnson, has developed an online assessment of retirement, "Retirement Success Profile," that is quite useful. The assessment and the training to use it can be accessed at http://www.retirementoptions.com. It explores 15 success factors for retirement:

1. Career Reorientation: Let Go. . .
2. Retirement Value: Reframe Your Attitudes. . .
3. Personal Empowerment: Take Charge. . .
4. Physical Wellness: Grow Well. . .
5. Monetary Adequacy: Find Your Wealth. . .
6. Quality of Life - Present: Seek Peace. . .
7. Quality of Life - Future: Have Dreams. . .
8. Spirituality/Meaning: Construct Purpose. . .
9. Respect for Leisure: Have Fun. . .
10. Personal Flexibility: Welcome Change. . .
11. Lifespan Spiritual Development: Live Now. . .
12. Care giving Responsibilities: Honor Yourself...
13. Home Life: Get Connected. . .
14. Maturation Vitality: Become Ageless. . .
15. Replacement of Work Functions: Get Going. . .

The report that is generated helps clients explore their retirement strengths and concerns, and develop a plan to bridge the two. Completion of a six-week teleclass training is required to administer this assessment to clients.

NOTES:

2. Retirement Satisfaction Inventory. An assessment of retirement satisfaction among nearly 400 individuals was administered by psychologists. Results were published in the Psychology of Aging journal of the American Psychological Association under the title "Assessing Retirement Satisfaction and Perceptions of Retirement Experiences." This tool examined the reasons for retirement, as well as satisfaction of retirees with their current situation. It may also be a useful tool for pre-retirees to identify areas of dissatisfaction that can be addressed both before and in retirement. The tool is reproduced in the Retirement Coaches Toolbox as Tool 20 (page 186) for your convenience.

NOTES:

3. Dr. Nancy Schlossberg. In *Retire Smart Retire Happy,* author Dr. Nancy Schlossberg provides a number of self-assessments for retirees to use in analyzing where they are in the process, their identity and internal resources, their relationships and social resources, four types of retirement personalities and "paths," overall resources and responses to change, and an overall questionnaire called "Your Future Quiz" that overviews expectations, transition, satisfaction, and how to make retirement "the time of your life." The book is just $14.95 USD and available through the American Psychological Association at http://www.apa.org/books/lifetools.html

NOTES:

4. Sedlar/Miners Quiz. *Don't Retire, Rewire* by Jeri Sedlar and Rick Miners contains some insightful self-assessments to (a) help clients determine whether retirement will be stressful for them, examining psychological preparation (or lack thereof), time-fulfilling activities, and change in family dynamics, (b) help clients determine their "drivers," or "the things that turn you on and make you tick as a person," and that may have been fulfilled by work up to now but must also be met in retirement. They list 30 primary drivers and help people develop retirement options that satisfy them.

NOTES:

5. **Retirement Stress Inventory.** A tool patterned after the widely used Holmes/Rahe stress assessment is the Retirement Stress Inventory available in the e-book, The Psychology of Retirement, published by BPTI Press 1999 and available for purchase at http://www.bpri.com/psycofrethow.html. The tool asks clients to review a list of 20 events and state whether the event either did not occur, occurred and was tolerable, or occurred and was not tolerable. The total score determines the client's level of retirement stress and whether or not coaching or counseling is indicated.

NOTES:

6. **Application of Other Assessments to Retirement.** Coaches who are already trained in other assessments may find them appropriate to retiring clients as well. These may include:

- Myers-Briggs Type Indicator,® available through http://www.cpp.com for overall personality style;
- MAPP assessment, available free at http://www.assessment.com to help retirees clarify interests
- Personal Interests, Attitudes and Values (PIAV), available through http://www.ttidisc.com (and for CCI/RCI coaches, through http://www.careercoachinstitute.com and http://www.retirementcoachinstitute.com) to help clients determine underlying motivators
- Self-Directed Search, available for $9.95 through http://www.self-directed-search.com/
- DiSC assessment, available at http://www.inscapepublishing.com, for insights into clients' behavioral profile

NOTES:

KEY CONCEPTS LEARNED:

10. VARIETIES OF RETIREMENT LIFESTYLES

"Don't simply retire from something; have something to retire to."
— Harry Emerson Fosdick

Learning Objectives:

1. Explore varieties of retirement lifestyles
2. Bring lessons from prior chapters it together to help clients plan a satisfying retirement lifestyle

Review of Chapter 9:

1. What is the biggest trap retirees face regarding their leisure time?

2. What should the retirement coach ask clients when they say they want to travel indefinitely in retirement?

3. What was your favorite assessment tool of those we discussed last week (including those in the Toolbox)? Why?

Elements of a Retirement Life

In the preceding chapters, we have explored a wide range of elements that are key to retirement planning, including:

- Elements of the Authentic Retirement model:
    1. Life purpose
    2. Values
    3. Motivators and interests
    4. Talents
    5. Experience
    6. Desired activities
    7. Lifestyle and environment
    8. Finances
- Emotional adjustments (transition, overall attitude, fear, boredom)
- Work issues and options
- New identity in retirement
- Aging realities, myths and fears
- Health

- Social/relationship shifts
- Leisure
- Education
- Travel
- Relocating

It is now time to bring all of this together and consider the various types of retirement lifestyles people might create. Of course, in theory there are literally thousands of ways to combine the above factors, but those listed below are representative.

The Retirement Lifestyle Template,™ Tool 21 in the Retirement Coaches Toolbox (page 190), can be used as clients complete worksheets provided earlier in this book and course, and at this point to summarize their desired lifestyle elements and mix. In this tool, clients indicate whether or not they feel prepared as to each of the aspects of retirement planning, and then list current and proposed additional activities that would fulfill each element.

Creativity and so-called "out of the box" thinking will be critical at this juncture. If there was ever a time not to settle for less than what one desires, retirement should be it! Even if financial resources are only average, focusing on key elements for quality of life and bringing that into being can significantly enhance enjoyment for the retiree.

Examples

Example 1 – Les

Les was a successful CEO with a long career in the software industry, age 60. His goal is to retire within the next two years. He wants to live in Chicago where he has lived for the past 15 years for half of each year, and in Florida the rest of the year. He is married and in good health, and has two grown children, one has a son who is 8 years old. He is achievement-motivated. His passion when not working is sailing. He has saved for 20 years toward retirement and has accumulated $3 million in investments, diversified into real estate, stock mutual funds, and stocks. Les and his wife enjoy traveling.

Les's Retirement Lifestyle Profile

Summary of desired lifestyle: I have an active retirement lifestyle. I jog daily, spend time with my wife, and sail as often as I can. I volunteer on the board of my local homeowners association, am treasurer for my local sailing club, and attend church regularly. I split my time between Boca Raton, Florida and Chicago during the year, alternated with sailing trips of 2-10 weeks at a time. I am comfortable financially and enjoy my life.

Proposed retirement date: January 1, 2006.

Purpose fulfilled: My life purpose is to lead with integrity and to cherish others, through all of the activities of and relationships in my life.

Values actualized: My primary values are independence, achievement, variety, and personal growth.

Motivators met: Achievement, creative outlet

Talents used: Leadership, working with my hands, mentoring, budgeting, teambuilding, rapport-building

Experience drawn upon: Increasingly responsible management positions within major software companies; 30 years of sailing; 35-year marriage

Desired activities to be pursued: 35% leisure, 10% personal time, 10% volunteering, 15% sailing, 15% time with spouse, family, 15% travel

Environment/lifestyle: I will live 6 months in Chicago, 6 months in Florida, with visits to other destinations of my choosing. My desired pace is moderate but not stressed, and I like feeling the support of my family and close friends.

Financial status: I believe my $3 million in assets is adequate for my retirement needs, so I will not need to work.

Anticipated barriers: The only barrier might be that my wife does not enjoy sailing all that much, but she will go with me on shorter trips. Also, my children have become financially dependent on our paying for some of their expenses, and I would like to terminate that without hurting their feelings.

How barriers will be overcome: I will find other friends that I can go sailing with, or intersperse sailing with other activities during our trips. And within the next 3 months I will sit down with each of my children and discuss how they can become more responsible for their own finances.

What would the primary coaching issues be for Les?

Example 2 – Doris

Doris is 63 and within one year of retirement. She is divorced and has worked for the state government for 25 years. She is vested in her pension plan. Her health is compromised by fibromyalgia, but she has been able to keep working since her diagnosis 5 years ago. She is afraid of being lonely in retirement, and has not pursued any hobbies due to her illness.

Doris's Retirement Lifestyle Profile

Summary of desired lifestyle: I am financially set for a conservative retirement, and plan to live in my current home and do as well as I can given my illness. I go to church weekly and watch the soaps on television.

Proposed retirement date: July 1, 2005.

Purpose fulfilled: My life purpose is to be healthy and help others to preserve their health.

Values actualized: My primary values are security, compensation, and friendship

Motivators met: I am motivated by consistency and predictability, and expect that to be fulfilled in my retirement.

Talents used: Able to enjoy the moment, carry out a routine, follow instructions, and clean house.

Experience drawn upon: I have lived alone for 10 years so am used to that. I can draw on my experience with fibromyalgia to help others.

Desired activities to be pursued: 25% television, 10% cooking, 25% resting, 5% walking or swimming (when I am able), 10% church, 10% seeing friends, 15% email and online classes.

Environment/lifestyle: I will live in the home I own, and prefer a slow pace of life.

Financial status: I can sustain myself for up to 20 years if I keep my living expenses below $2000 per month.

Anticipated barriers: I cannot get medical insurance due to my illness, so major hospitalization before I am 65 could wipe out my assets. I also see my illness as a barrier and fear loneliness.

How barriers will be overcome: I can continue to explore options for insurance and try to save money for health care (though that will be hard when I'm not working!). I will also continue to become more educated about fibromyalgia, and see if some of the eastern medicine can help. I will try to get out and meet people as my health permits.

What would the primary coaching issues be if you were working with Doris?

Example 3 – Jim

Jim is 68 and still working. He has been unable to retire because half of his retirement savings were wiped out in the 2001 stock market crash and he has been unable to recoup them. He has had many jobs during his career in manufacturing, from assembly line worker in an automobile manufacturer to shop foreman (currently) for a medium-sized company that makes boats. He is married, and his wife works part-time as secretary for their church. He has current assets of $250,000 and expects to continue working indefinitely. However, arthritis is starting to impact his ability to do his job. He lives in a small Midwest town near his son John, who is single.

Jim's Retirement Lifestyle Profile

Summary of desired lifestyle: I am happily "retired," by my own definition, which involves less work than I'm doing now and more time to pursue my hobby of racing radio-controlled cars. My wife and I enjoy spending more time together and doing things with our son. I use my handy skills around the house to fix things and on projects I enjoy. I'm involved in the local radio controlled car club and spend time every week on my hobby. We take driving trips when my wife can get time off, but otherwise stick pretty close to home.

Proposed retirement date: Not planned; may go to part time work in a couple of years

Purpose fulfilled: My life purpose is to do the most with what I have throughout my life activities and relationships.

Values actualized: My primary values are financial security, structure, and family values.

Motivators met: I am motivated by seeing the tangible results of my work and seeing my investments grow.

Talents used: Mechanical skills, fixing things

Experience drawn upon: My years in the manufacturing industry and our long-term marriage.

Desired activities to be pursued: 35% working, 25% household projects, 25% with wife and family, 5% managing my investments, 10% personal time

Environment/lifestyle: I will live in the moderate home we bought years ago; I can't afford to move nor can I think of anywhere else I'd like to live.

Financial status: I think we will be ok if my wife keeps working and I can stay with this job full-time for two more years and save a lot. We will minimize our expenses and avoid luxury items.

Anticipated barriers: Money is the main one, and my health could prevent me from working as long as I need to financially. I have health insurance, but not disability or long-term care insurance.

How barriers will be overcome: Not sure, guess we'll just do what we can! If my wife has to increase her hours and income, that might be another possibility.

What would the primary coaching issues be for Jim?

KEY CONCEPTS LEARNED:

11. THE RETIRING WORKFORCE: ANOTHER SIDE OF THE RETIREMENT WAVE

"By working faithfully eight hours a day, you may eventually get to be a boss and work twelve hours a day."
– Robert Frost

Learning Objectives:

1. Clarify some of the primary issues and questions employers must face as the Baby Boomers retire
2. Discuss how organizations must respond in order to survive the effects of the retiring workforce

Review of Chapter 10:

How can you help clients gain an overall picture of their desired retirement lifestyle and any barriers?

Issues for Employers of Retiring Boomers

As nearly half of the Baby Boomers employed by the U.S. Government become eligible to retire in the next two years, and the rest of the cohort the 15 years following that, employers will face a whole new set of issues! Some retirement coaches will be retained to work directly with management of corporations in industries highly affected by talent loss through retiring workers; others will encounter this issue when working with individual pre-retirees as they describe their work context. This week we discuss the issues organizations must face.

Lack of Employer Awareness

Many organizations can become their own worst enemy if they have remained unaware of the significance of the talent shortage, and that it is looming right around the corner. Awareness of the issue is a prerequisite to resolution. In *Impending Crisis,* an insightful treatment of this topic, authors Roger Herman et al state:

> *"The Impending Crisis is a dangerously critical shortage of qualified people to perform the work of employer organizations. What we will experience in 2003-2010 will make the workforce talent crisis of the late 1990's seem like a practice session."*

Figure 16 illustrates this shortage:

Impending Crisis: Skilled Labor Shortage

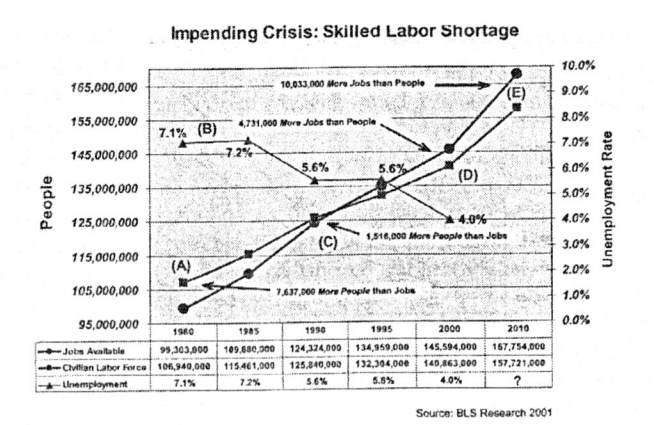

	1980	1985	1990	1995	2000	2010
Jobs Available	99,303,000	109,680,000	124,324,000	134,959,000	145,594,000	167,754,000
Civilian Labor Force	106,940,000	115,461,000	125,840,000	132,304,000	140,863,000	157,721,000
Unemployment	7.1%	7.2%	5.6%	5.6%	4.0%	?

Source: BLS Research 2001

Figure 9: Impending Crisis: Skilled Labor Shortage
This chart illustrates three trends in U.S. employment from 1980 to 2010: the civilian labor force, the approximate number of jobs available, and the unemployment rate. The historical and projected employment data is drawn from research by the U.S. Bureau of Labor Statistics. In 1980, the United States had approximately 7,637,000 more people available to work than there were jobs available (A). The unemployment rate in 1980 was 7.1 percent (B). By 1990, the employment condition had changed, but there were still approximately 1,516,000 more people available to work than there were jobs available (C). In 1994, the employment condition reversed itself for the first time in U.S. history where there were now more jobs available than there were people available to work. By 2000, there were 4,731,000 more jobs available than there were people able to work and the unemployment rate nationwide was 4.0 percent (D). The 2010 projection is that the U.S. employment market will have 10,033,000 more jobs available than there will be people to fill them (E).

To clarify further: the "crisis" will be a shortage of *qualified* people to hire, not just warm bodies as was common in the 1990's. Fueled in large part by the mass exodus of retiring Baby Boomers (76 million people born between 1946 and 1964), the Bureau of Labor Statistics forecasts a shortage of 10,033,000 workers by 2010. *But this is not the whole picture!* The next generation of workers that will replace the boomers, those born between 1965 and 1983 (better known as Generation Xers) number only 66 million people. The entire demographic debacle must be considered. No industry will escape the impact and no employer will be immune to it. As employers become aware of the impending crisis, they go through typical stages, according to Herman et al:

Stage 1: No Clue. (25 percent of employers) They're responding to the workforce "weather" of day-to-day operations and job postings and not noticing the broader "climate" – many of this group are in denial that a problem has begun.

Stage 2: Awareness. (50 percent of employers) They know there may be some sort of labor shortage, agree it's sometimes difficult to find the right person for a job.

The people who work for the managers and execs in such companies are often more aware than their bosses, which is frustrating for them.

Stage 3: Appreciation, Preliminary Understanding. (20 percent of total) These people are highly concerned about the labor shortage, feel moved to do something about it.

Stage 4: Comprehensive Understanding, Internalization. (5 percent of total) They know their human resources are clearly their most valuable resource and are great places to work.

There is some controversy about how extensive the shortage will be. For example, see http://www.workforce.com

NOTES:

Roots of Early Retirement

The early retirement of many workers is expected to expedite the impact of the Boomers on the employment crisis, employers must understand the reasons for this new trend before forming any solutions. A major reason is due to downsizings and *the way that people were handled* that changed the model of work and resulted in bad feelings. Companies were selfish and took the "revolving door" approach. Many workers lost their middle class lifestyle. The workforce became lean, and long hours became the norm. Older workers were often targeted for layoffs. New workers, temps and consultants were brought in to replace older workers who could have been retrained. And the trust that had existed between employee and employer was broken. These workers will be reluctant to return to those same companies later.

NOTES:

Employer versus Retiree Needs: a Disconnect

Employers will need highly qualified, high energy, full time people. And they may need them to have education, experience, or other qualifications that they do not have.

As we have seen, many older workers will prefer part-time, contract, temporary, or flexible work schedules. Unless employers change their practices, retirees will leave these companies with valuable expertise and will not be able to be re-employed by that firm – and no one else is waiting in the wings to take their place.

According to a research study entitled performed by the *Center for Organizational Research*:

The sectors that will be affected by retiring Boomers most are:

- Government
- Education
- Manufacturing
- Transportation
- Healthcare (especially hospitals)

The occupations that will be most affected are:

- Executive, administrative and managerial positions
- Professional jobs requiring high levels of education
- Jobs in unionized environments
- Jobs in industries where downsizing or hiring freezes skewed age distribution
- Part-time jobs

What older workers will choose to do most often in post retirement:. According to a recent AARP study:

- Customer service rep
- Teaching assistant
- Teacher
- Retail salesperson
- Landscaper or groundskeeper
- Cashier
- Computer support specialist
- Real estate agent
- Secretary or receptionist
- Truck driver or courier
- Bookkeeper or accounting clerk
- Childcare worker

But these needs do not match well with projected needs of employers, who may require highly skilled laborers and not be able to find qualified individuals to fill those positions.

NOTES:

The Discrimination Issue

The question here is, will employers come to terms with the new majority of "older workers"? The new definition of "older worker" is over 40. In the mid 1990's, the largest portion of the workforce was in its late 20's to late 30's. By 2002, (less than 10 years later) that age range had shifted to the late 30's to late 40's. Many hiring managers may feel that people over 40 are not as creative or productive as younger workers and therefore are not worth training.

The Costs of Hiring

Competition for scarce talent will drive recruiting, hiring and salary costs to new highs. Already, cost to train a new employee is 100 to 150 percent of the annual salary for many positions. Supply and demand economics will drive the cost of human capital. Bidding wars can become dangerous, cutting profitability and producing inflation.

Appealing to Generation X

Will organizations be technologically savvy enough to attract the new Gen-X "techno-wizards"? Growing up with television and taking to computers and the Internet like a fish to water, these workers can be a tremendous asset to organizations. But will Boomers be jealous? Were the "tech-impaired" Boomers an asset after all? Will the Gen-Xer's be overqualified? Will employers be able to challenge them? What about the next generation called *the Millennials* (those born after 1985)? How will they deal with them?

Another issue pertaining to Gen-X employees is: Can they be trained "your way"? In 2001, a survey of 32-year-old workers revealed that their average number of jobs held was 8.6. Corporate loyalty is gone and is being replaced by "loyalty to oneself." Gen-Xer's will not follow the paths of being managed as their downsized Boomer parents did, by working long days and taking orders from "the boss." In an effort to control their own destiny, they will seek companies who can offer them life-work balance. But are they less flexible than older workers?

And even if these two obstacles can be overcome, there are millions less of workers in the Generation X cohort than in the Boomer cohort, which is bound to leave many positions still unfilled, say some.

NOTES:

The Employer Response

How can organizations survive the impact of the "Impending Crisis"? if you had a client company who understood the importance of the Impending Crisis and wanted to get started, what do they do? Here are the steps in the "Checklist to Get Started" from Herman et al:

1. Arrange for everyone on the company's strategic team to read *Impending Crisis*.
2. Determine which of the four stages of awareness the company is at now. Evaluate how much time it will take to get the company "competent" considering these typical/possible time lines:
    a. Small companies: 18 months
    b. Medium-sized companies: 2 to 3 years
    c. Large companies: 3 to 5 years
3. Have the client schedule a meeting soon to discuss seriously what they have learned and how the evolving crisis will affect his/her organization. This meeting should be held off-site to avoid interruptions.
4. In this and subsequent meetings, encourage the client to creatively examine every aspect of the way they do business; challenge everything. Use an outside facilitator if needed to avoid personal agendas.
5. Have each strategic-level player bring his/her management team into the game. Re-create the organization and its processes. Don't be afraid to question whether the objective(s) are even worthwhile.
6. Begin to engage the rest of the company's employees, making the engagement very positive. Avoid any associations of this process with the infamous reengineering fad. Don't expect the transformation to happen overnight; it won't and it shouldn't.

Another excellent treatment of the employer side of the retirement wave – complete with examples of how major companies have begun to address the issues – is *Age Wave: What Corporate America Must Do to Survive the Graying of the Workforce*, by Beverly Goldberg. Goldberg suggests that people retire from work early and that younger people dislike large companies are: (1) how downsizings have been handled (taking people by surprise with the announcement and overworking the remaining workers, (2) the current retirement norm as it is evolving, and (3) discrimination both in hiring and during employment.

What is needed, the author suggests, is to address these issues so that workers will remain employed longer or return to work (perhaps on a modified basis). Recommended steps are:

- Address the causes of worker stress and anxiety
- Establish corporate communications programs to provide realistic, useful information

- Develop a mission statement and action plan to help corporations rebuild their reputations (and the trust of their employees()
- Develop flexible work structures
- Offer training and retraining programs
- Incorporate diversity programs
- Make benefits portable

A study of over 2700 human resource managers by the Society of Human Resource Management and the AARP found:

- 62 percent said they hire retired employees as consultants
- 47 percent provide training to upgrade older worker skills
- 29 percent provide opportunities for workers to transfer to jobs with reduced pay and responsibilities
- 19 percent have a phased retirement program that gradually reduces work schedules
- 10 percent provide alternative career tracks for older workers

This falls far short of where companies will need to be to remain competitive and productive in the coming years!

AARP has a program called the Senior Community Service Employment Program (SCSEP) designed to provide temporary work experience assignments for people age 55 and over whose incomes fall at or below the federal poverty line. Enrollees are given temporary assignments with nonprofit community organizations (host agencies) where they have an opportunity to sharpen and develop skills while searching for a permanent job.

The goal of the program is for each of its enrollees to gain the skills necessary to find employment outside of the program. The AARP SCSEP program is funded by the U.S. Department of Labor under the authority of the Older Americans Act of 1965. AARP SCSEP has 90 project sites and is located in 31 states and Puerto Rico.

Eligible applicants are placed in nonprofit or public/community service agencies where they receive on-the-job training for at least 20 hours per week. They are paid at least the current minimum wage. During their temporary assignments, enrollees work with the director of the local SCSEP project to locate permanent part-time or full-time employment.

Enrollees benefit from the AARP SCSEP in many ways, such as getting help in developing job search skills and in locating a permanent job; getting paid work experience to improve job skills and develop new ones; an opportunity to establish a current work history and an up-to-date resume; paid sick leave; paid holidays; worker's compensation insurance; a yearly physical examination; a one-year complimentary AARP membership; and training opportunities.

For additional resources, see also http://www.employerofchoice.com, which offers formal recognition for employers who qualify. This designation significantly strengthens a company's posture to attract talent and business partners. Also visit http://www.impendingcrisis.com

See also the suggestions by Ken Dychtwald in, "It's Time to Retire Retirement" (see Resource List).

NOTES:

KEY CONCEPTS LEARNED:

12. FILLING YOUR RETIREMENT COACHING PRACTICE

> "I don't know the key to success, but the key to failure is trying to please everybody."
> – Bill Cosby

Learning Objectives:

1. Discover what questions to ask to clarify your retirement coaching niche
2. Learn a variety of proven strategies to use in marketing your retirement coaching services
3. Challenge yourself with new ways to fill your practice

Review of Chapter 11:

1. What are some of the main issues and questions employers must face as the Baby Boomers retire?

2. What are three strategies organizations need to consider in order to survive the effects of the retiring workforce?

A 10-Step Plan for Marketing Retirement Coaching

To be successful in marketing yourself as a retirement coach, you will want to use all steps of the GEMS™ [Generating and Executing a Marketing Strategy – that Works!] Approach outlined in Figure 17. Please look at this roadmap now (it appears on the next page); and we will discuss each step. For more detail on starting and growing your coaching practice, visit http://www.6figurecoach.com.

1. Define what kind of retirement coach you want to be. While we can say we are "specializing" by focusing on retirement issues. But that does not adequately define our niche!

    a. Brand. How would you define your personal brand and niche? Will you use a particular assessment or approach? Target a certain age group, geographic region, industry, or other demographics?

Figure 17: THE GEMS™ APPROACH TO MARKETING

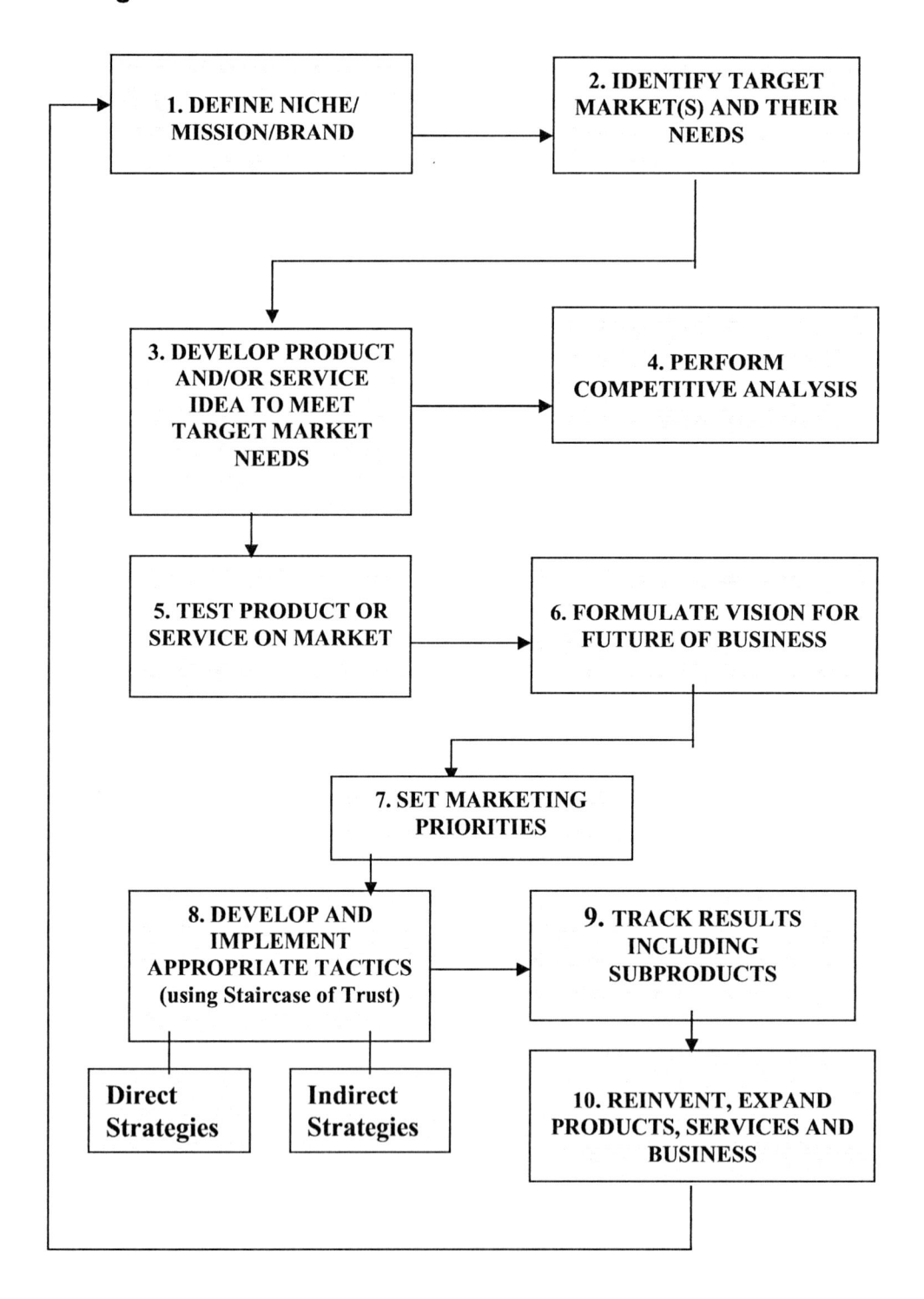

1. DEFINE NICHE/MISSION/BRAND → 2. IDENTIFY TARGET MARKET(S) AND THEIR NEEDS → 3. DEVELOP PRODUCT AND/OR SERVICE IDEA TO MEET TARGET MARKET NEEDS → 4. PERFORM COMPETITIVE ANALYSIS

3. → 5. TEST PRODUCT OR SERVICE ON MARKET → 6. FORMULATE VISION FOR FUTURE OF BUSINESS → 7. SET MARKETING PRIORITIES → 8. DEVELOP AND IMPLEMENT APPROPRIATE TACTICS (using Staircase of Trust) → 9. TRACK RESULTS INCLUDING SUBPRODUCTS → 10. REINVENT, EXPAND PRODUCTS, SERVICES AND BUSINESS → (back to 1)

8. → Direct Strategies; Indirect Strategies

b. **Target market(s).** Ideally you will want three target markets with opposite economic cycles to smooth out your cash flow. Launching one every six months often works well. How would you define your primary, secondary, and third target markets?

c. **Positioning against "competitors".** Good branding eliminates the competition. Do you know the other providers/coaches that your clients may also be considering? How can you identify them? How do you compare? (See *Discover Your Niche* by Marcia Bench in Resource List for detailed competitive analysis form.)

> **NOTE:** You must consider three different kinds of competitors in your analysis: a) those offering a smaller range of services than you, b) those offering similar range, and c) those offering a larger range than you

2. **Determine what products and services you will offer.**
    a. **Develop working hypothesis.** You may know you want to offer retirement coaching, perhaps using the standard 90-day commitment meeting once a week. But what other products might you also offer? Assessments, workbooks, networking group? How will you package your services? Packaging your services along with related products increases the value of every sale and creates a perception of added value.

    b. **Perform a market test to ensure your ideas match those of your target clients.** Market testing will validate or counter your working hypothesis. A formal or informal survey of people similar to (or actual) prospective clients can be useful, using a web administration tool such as http://www.surveymonkey.com or another tool. Using your success team or peer group can also help provide additional perspectives.

3. **Develop a vision for your ideal practice.**

A vision statement must not only articulate the logical aspects of your ideal coaching business (income, list of services, etc.); it must also tap into your *emotions.* What would be wonderfully exciting for you to achieve? How will it *feel* when you reach your goals? What kind of feedback will you get from your clients? Write a description of your vision as though it were a technicolor movie, vivid and clear.

4. **Use the Internet to build awareness.**
    a. **Your own web site.** Use metatags, titles, and content that highlight retirement coaching and any important aspects of your niche. Software

such as http://www.wordtracker.com can help you choose the best search terms to use in your titles, metatags, and text.

    b. **Web link exchanges.** Exchange links with complementary resources so that you both benefit from the exposure. This will raise your rankings in the search engines, increasing the likelihood that people will find you.

    c. **Coach directories.** Sites such as http://www.coachfederation.org, http://www.careercoachinstitute.com, and http://www.coachvillereferral.com offer coaching directories that are searchable by expertise – you can be one of the few coaches focusing on retirement!

    d. **Pay per click (use with caution!).** You can sign up for services that drive web traffic to you when a particular term is searched or clicked on from a specific location. Just be cautious – novices can lose significant dollars when using this strategy without proper guidance or knowledge.

5. **Start an ezine – and write articles for others.**
    a. **Gather your contacts/mailing list – and continue to aggregate it!** Use http://www.1shoppingcart.com , http://www.aweber.com , http://www.constantcontact.com or similar services. Your money is in your database!
    b. **Write a Top 10 list to use as a giveaway or to place in other ezines.** The top 10 lists at http://www.topten.org/ can serve as examples. Notice the format and topic choice of those listed, then develop your own (e.g., "Top 10 Keys to Successful Retirement").
    c. For details on how to start and manage your email newsletter, or ezine, we recommend Karon Thackston's ebook entitled *The Step by Step Guide to Creating and Promoting Your Ezine* found here http://www.creatingezines.com/

We recommend that you also write articles and participate in chat groups for such sites as:
- Thirdage.com
- USBoomers.com
- Retirementwithapurpose.com
- Notyetretired.com
- Ideamarketers.com

Contact these sites to find out how to place an on-line advertisement promoting your coaching service.

Write articles/place advertisement in local newspapers and business journals, and magazines geared to retirees.

6. Give teleclasses and speak at service and professional groups. We recommend the teleleader training at http://www.teleclassinternational.com to learn how to present classes over the phone, and for in-person speaking, the National Speakers Association at http://www.nsaspeaker.org/ (including its local chapters) and Toastmasters, http://www.toastmasters.com/.

Groups you might speak to on retirement coaching could be found in the Yellow Pages for your area under "Associations" or in directories of associations (available at your local library) which list them by budget, industry/ies they serve, whether or not they have local or national conferences, publications, and the like.

Or if you have targeted a specific industry, speak or network at affiliated associations i.e. airline industry, teachers, human resource, doctors, attorneys (whatever industry you might have been associated within your prior career).

Then integrate these and articles into the "Staircase of Trust" described here:

The Staircase Of Trust
[adapted from *Fill Your Practice* by Marcia Bench]

Following is an example of a sequence of marketing tactics – which we call the Staircase of Trust – that we have tested and proven to be successful in generating an ongoing flow of qualified leads to a coaching business. Notice how the level of both risk and commitment increases with each step.

- Launch a web site that points immediately to the emotional benefits of your service and suggests that you have a solution to your target market's "hot buttons," or emotional needs (e.g., emotional pain, confusion, frustration, lack of money/fear, etc.)
- Get your web site well-placed on the major search engines (consult your web site designer, web hosting company, or an internet consultant).
- Invite the web site visitor to opt in to your ezine that further addresses their needs to ensure that you are adding these people to your database for future promotions
- Offer a free report to the visitor/prospect, either without further commitment or as your gift if they purchase your book
- Offer a free teleclass or e-course in which you preview your brand of coaching – and have it taped (our vendor of choice is Audio Strategies http://www.audiostrategies.com) and uploaded to your web site for visitors to hear at their convenience
- At the free teleclass, offer a discount on a four-session paid teleclass, a paid live seminar, or 90 days of coaching services

- Once a client commits to coaching or paid training, request referrals from them initially and at specified intervals; share success stories (with client permission) in your ezine so that others can learn more about the work you do
- Also share these success stories as examples in future seminars, books, your company brochure, and with the media (again, always with client permission, as required by International Coach Federation Ethical Standards at http://www.coachfederation.org) to gain further exposure for your practice.

7. Cultivate referrals through strategic alliances with financial planners, estate planners, and marriage & family therapists. Target those who specialize in the mid-life population, or other coaches who specialize in other areas. Workshops can be held in community association clubhouses, senior centers or even on cruise ships. Promote their services to your clients, and ask them to promote your services to theirs.

8. Develop relationships with and coverage by local and national media. Assemble a press kit which includes some or all of the following:

- Brochure, if any, about you and your practice
- Copies of any articles you have written and had published (on high quality white paper or, ideally, color photocopy
- Fact Sheet about coaching from which the writer or editor can excerpt
- Interview angles or ideas for interviewers to use
- Photo of you (black and white glossy)
- Bio (if not included in the brochure)
- List of past sponsors, clients, or other people and organizations with whom you have worked (if not included in brochure)
- Press release about the event that provides the "hook" you want them to use – an upcoming event, etc.

Learn to write newsworthy press releases; if you don't know how, use a professional copywriter such as Karon Thackston (http://www.marketingwords.com) or a publicist (expensive but worth it when you're doing a new product launch or big event!).

9. Track your efforts and results; set and re-set priorities. The Retirement Coaches Toolbox contains a checklist on page 195 of a whole host of marketing strategies and gives you a chance to decide which you will use and in what order you will use them. By tracking not only ultimate outcome (usually revenue), but also how your clients find you, how many contacts it takes until you make a sale (and they become your client or purchase one of your products), you can calculate time and cost per customer and become more efficient in your marketing. Turn to this worksheet now; how many of these strategies are things you had not thought of yet?

10. Expand your practice. As your ideas evolve, you may wish to write a book, develop an extended paid seminar, license or franchise your approach, create and sell a kit of materials, and/or use other expansion strategies to meet your goals. See *Fill Your Practice* and http://www.6figurecoach.com for other ideas.

NOTES:

KEY CONCEPTS LEARNED:

CONTENTS OF RETIREMENT COACHES TOOLBOX

1.	Retirement Readiness Wheel	141
2.	Ideal Retirement Exercise	142
3.	Authentic Retirement Worksheet No. 1: Life Purpose	143
4.	Authentic Retirement Worksheet No. 2: Values	146
5.	Authentic Retirement Worksheet No. 3: Motivators & Interests	149
6.	Authentic Retirement Worksheet No. 4: Talents	152
7.	Authentic Retirement Worksheet No. 5: Experience	154
8.	Authentic Retirement Worksheet No. 6: Desired Activities	157
9.	Authentic Retirement Worksheet No. 7: Environment	160
10.	Authentic Retirement Worksheet No. 8: Finance Factor	163
11.	My Beliefs About Money	165
12.	Coper/Thriver Quiz	167
13.	Coaching Questions for Each Thriver Cluster	170
14.	Should I Work in Retirement?	172
15.	Is Entrepreneurship Right For You?	173
16.	My Retirement Health	174
17.	Top Ten Indicators to Refer to a Mental Health Professional	176
18.	My Social Network	180
19.	What Will I Do With My Time?	182
20.	Retirement Satisfaction Inventory	186
21.	Retirement Lifestyle Template	190
22.	My Retirement Lifestyle Profile	194
23.	Marketing Priorities Checklist	195
24.	Resource List for Retirement Coaches	198

RETIREMENT COACHES TOOLBOX

1. Retirement Readiness Wheel

To determine how ready you are to retire, please indicate your level of satisfaction with each of the areas forming spokes of the wheel below (7 = most satisfied, 1 = least satisfied).

Retirement Readiness Wheel
Prepare for Authentic Retirement™

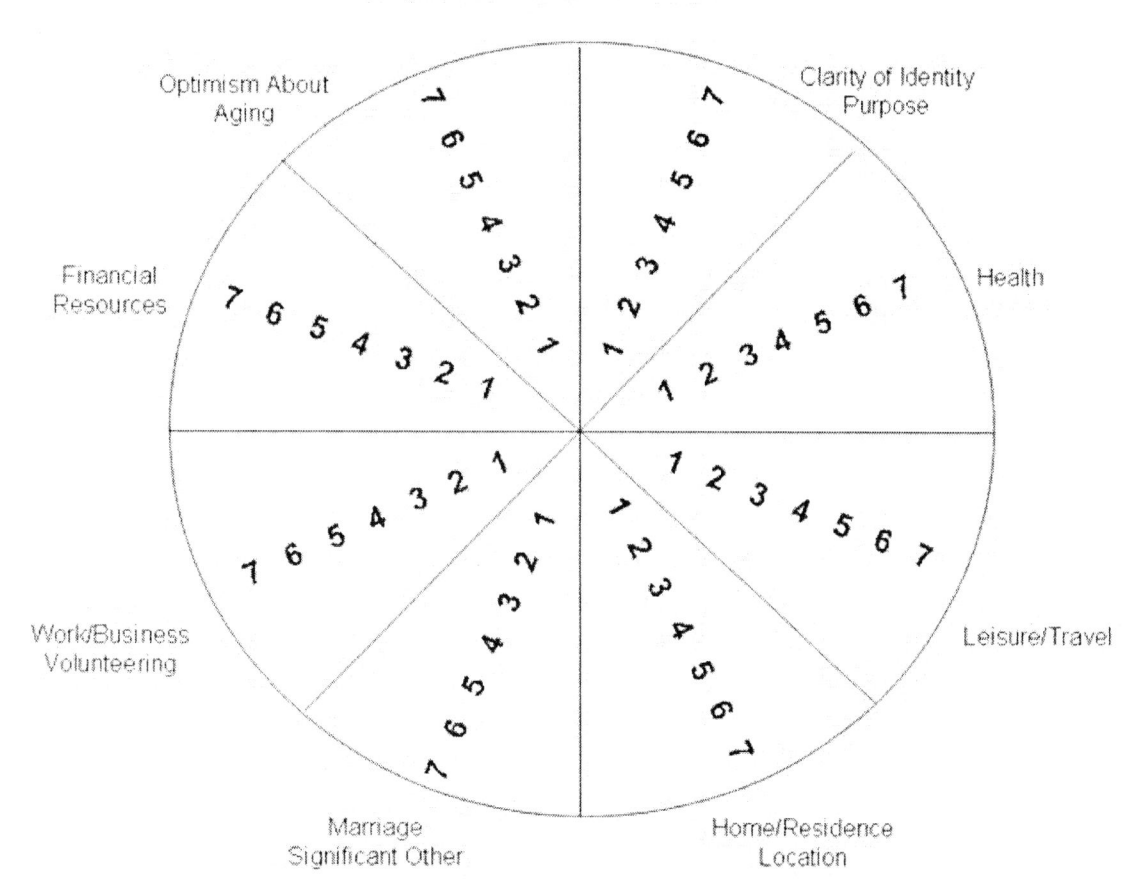

Spokes: Optimism About Aging, Clarity of Identity/Purpose, Health, Leisure/Travel, Home/Residence Location, Marriage/Significant Other, Work/Business Volunteering, Financial Resources.

Copyright © Marcia Bench 2004

Now, imagine the numbers you chose connecting to form a wheel. The rounder the wheel, the more balanced your retirement life. Imagine how your car would travel if the wheels were in this shape! Are you content with the balance? If not, a coach can help.

2. Ideal Retirement Exercise

Imagine that you are writing a movie script which depicts a day in your ideal retired life. You must describe every detail of the scenery, your feelings, and your activities, as well as the people with whom you are interacting. Describe it in such vivid form that a producer (someone besides you!) could read your description and instruct others in building the props, casting the characters, bringing the right personality and style to the acting, and sequence the activities the actors are doing! Include your work, your home, your family life, your leisure activities, any special aspects in your environment, the pace, and each activity you do from dawn till bedtime. Imagine there are no restrictions in time, money, or any other aspect. Ready? Write that description in the space below, on a separate sheet, or on your computer. Take 10 to 20 minutes to do this.

3. Authentic Retirement Worksheet No. 1: Life Purpose

The Authentic Retirement Process is designed to provide a focus for your retirement from concept to implementation. Please work through it thoughtfully, taking your time, and allowing your unique gifts and your true self to emerge as you do.

We begin by exploring the first element of your Authentic Retirement, Life Purpose. Find a quiet place and about an hour of undisturbed time, and respond to each of the following questions.

Clue No. 1: What do you love to do when you have spare time?

Clue No. 2: What parts of your present job or life activities do you thoroughly enjoy? .

Clue No. 3: What do you naturally do well?

Clue No. 4: What have been your 10 greatest successes to date (in your eyes)?

Success	What Makes It a Success for You
1.	
2.	

3.	
4.	
5.	
6.	
7.	
8.	
9.	
10.	

Clue No. 5: Is there a cause or value or quality which you feel passionate about?

Clue No. 6: What are the 10 most important lessons you have learned in your life?

Lesson	What Makes It Significant
1.	
2.	
3.	
4.	
5.	
6.	
7.	
8.	

9.	
10.	

Clue No. 7: Think back over your life. Are there some issues or perceived problems that have occurred over and over again?

Clue No. 8: What do you daydream (or dream) about doing?

Clue No. 9: Imagine you are writing your epitaph. What things do you want to be remembered for? What things will your life be incomplete without?

Clue No. 10: What would you do if you knew you could not fail?

Now, narrow down your responses to glean the 10 most important aspects of your life purpose and write any themes you notice here:

Themes

To compose your life's purpose statement, synthesizing your responses to the Clues, use the following format:

"My life's purpose is to_____[ESSENCE]_____ through [EXPRESSION]_____."

The *essence* portion is relatively unchanged through your life, as in "My life's purpose is to promote peace on earth." The *expression* portion changes as your life circumstances change, so it lists all of your activities and relationships.

Here is a sample of a complete life purpose statement:

> *"My life purpose is to increase the harmony and love in the world through volunteering in the local Big Brother/Big Sister program, using a harmonious communication approach in my relationships, pursuing peace in all of my personal and professional relationships, maintaining my personal mental and physical health, being involved in my church, and teaching my grandchildren to seek harmony instead of discord."*

Write your life's purpose statement here:

"My life's purpose is to _____ through _____ _____ _____."

4. Authentic Retirement Worksheet No. 2: Values

You are now ready to explore the second element of your Authentic Retirement, Values. For your retirement to be fulfilling, it must allow your most important values in life to be expressed.

Values can be identified by asking yourself, "What do I want out of my life?" "What standards are important to me in my relationships and activities?" Begin by asking yourself these questions now, and write down your responses.

My Critical Values

I want the following from life:

1.

2.

3.

4.

The most important criteria or standards for my relationships and activities are:

1.

2.

3.

4.

5.

Some values commonly expressed are listed below. Rank each of the listed values as (1) not important, (2) moderately important, or (3) very important to you in your choice of career.

___ Enjoyment (having fun at what you do)

___ Helping other people (in a direct way)

___ Friendships (developing close relationships with co-workers)

___ Helping society (contributing to the betterment of the world)

___ Freedom (flexible schedule, independence)

___ Recognition (being recognized in a tangible way)

___ Creativity (having opportunity to express your ideas and yourself; innovation)

___ Location (being able to live where you choose)

___ Competition (matching your abilities with others')

___ Power and authority (being in managerial or leadership position; being responsible for supervising others; having decisionmaking authority)

___ Achievement (accomplishing desired objective; mastery)

___ Compensation (receiving equivalent in value or effect for services rendered)

___ Variety (a mix of tasks to perform and people dealt with during each day)

___ Security (feeling of stability, no worry; certainty)

___ Prestige (being seen as successful; obtaining recognition and status)

___ Aesthetics (beauty of environment; contributing to beauty of the world)

___ Morality and ethics (living according to a code or set of rules; enhancing world ethics)

___ Intellectual stimulation (being in an environment that encourages and stimulates thinking)

___ Public contact (being around people, as opposed to being alone or working with objects only)

___ Pace (busy versus relaxed atmosphere)

___ Risk (monetary or other risks -- e.g., new product development or start-up enterprise)

___ Other: _____

Now, think about your current lifestyle. How many of the values you have marked "3" for "very important" are being fulfilled? Your answer gives you a very important insight as to why you may feel dissatisfied – or not quite ready to retire yet!

List your five most important values here (whether included in the above list or not):

1. _____

2. _____

3. _____

4. _____

5. _____

5. Authentic Retirement Worksheet No. 3: Motivators and Interests

It is important to understand what motivates you to do something so that your retirement lifestyle will satisfy these motivators. Many believe that making more money or getting better benefits will keep them motivated. Others believe full-time leisure is what they would like most. What motivates most of us in the long run are challenge, variety, creative self-expression, good friends to support us, and a sense of achievement. What is it that motivates you? The following exercise will help you answer this important question.

My Motivators

Think of at least four instances in which you felt highly motivated to do an activity, whether in a job, school, a hobby, or some other type of situation. Describe them below:

1.

2.

3.

4.

Now, consider what each of these activities had in common. Were you in a similar setting? With similar types of people? Doing a particular kind of task you genuinely enjoy? Did you feel a certain way (e.g., challenged, proud, etc.)? List those common threads below:

These are some of the things that will motivate you in your retirement. Can you think of others? Add those to your list. Finally, list the five most important motivators that get you excited and/or dedicated to doing something.

Interests

Often, but *not* always, doing what interests us keeps us motivated. The categories examined in the Self-Directed Search, based on the work of Dr. John Holland, can give you clues to your interests. The six categories are:

  a. *Realistic* – prefers activities involving systematic manipulation of machinery, tools or animals; lack social skills
  b. *Investigative* – analytical, curious, methodical, and precise; lack leadership skills

c. *Artistic* – expressive, nonconforming, original, introspective; lack clerical skills
d. *Social* – enjoy working with and helping others; avoid ordered, systematic activities and lack mechanical/scientific ability
e. *Enterprising* – enjoy manipulating others to attain organizational goals or economic gain, avoid symbolic/systematic activities; lack scientific ability
f. *Conventional* – enjoy manipulating data in systematic way, filing records, and reproducing materials; avoid artistic activities

You can assess yourself by determining which of these descriptions fit you best, and to formally assess your interests using the Self-Directed Search yourself (which costs $9.95), at http://www.self-directed-search.com/ or see your coach.

6. Authentic Retirement Worksheet No. 4: Talents

You are now ready to explore the fourth element of your Authentic Retirement, Talents. During your work and life thus far, you have developed some skills through schooling, further honed your natural aptitudes, and learned others. What you are to primarily identify here is the things you know how to do that come naturally, rather than those you learned because a job required it.

In the spaces below, please place an x or checkmark next to the areas in which you have (W) work experience in that skill, (E) education using that skill, (M) managed people in that area, and (P) if you have a passion about it, consider it a natural talent, and would like to use it in retirement.

Talent Inventory

Talent or Skill	W	E	M	P
Multifunctional management				
Operations management				
Staff management				
Budgeting/finance				
Business/strategic planning				
Running my own business				
Labor relations				
Negotiations				
Accounting				
Bookkeeping				
Staff development				
Doing more with less				
Project management				
Product manufacturing				
Process engineering				
Computer systems design				
Software systems design, troubleshooting				
Computer programming				
Internet research				
Web site design				
Bidding/proposals				
Grant writing				
Non-profit start-up				
Tax return preparation				
Writing policies and procedures				
Answering telephones				
Screening calls/emails				
Sales				

Marketing				
Advertising				
Time management				
Customer relations				
Building rapport with others				
Research and development				
New product development				
Written communications				
Public speaking/presentations				
Curriculum development				
Quality control				
Shipping and receiving				
Cooking/baking				
Fixing/building things				
Spreadsheets/financial analysis				
Internet sales/purchasing				
Media relations				
Teaching/training				
Human resources				
Resume writing				
Coaching				
Consulting				
Interviewing				
Compensation and benefits				
Customizing products/services				
Fund raising				
Brochure design/graphic arts				
Teambuilding				
Facilities management				
Construction management				
Legal brief/document preparation				
Litigation				
Real estate negotiations, contracts				
Singing				
Reading music				
Copywriting				

If your talents are not listed in the worksheet, please write them in the blank spaces near the bottom.

Coaching Authentic Retirement

7. Authentic Retirement Worksheet No. 5: Life and Work Experience

You are now ready to explore the fifth factor of your Authentic Retirement, work and other experience. List your experience – including jobs, volunteer roles, committee memberships, and memorable family experiences or trips -- in your life to date in the space below.

Dates	Job/Activity/Role/Position

Place a * next to the experiences you enjoyed most in the above list.

Then, for each memorable experience listed, you will now need to write some Life Experience Stories. The three elements of a Life Experience Story are:
- Challenge or circumstance when you began the project or task
- Action you took to create a result or solve a problem
- Result that followed, quantified whenever possible

Here is an example of a Life Experience Story in the work context:

Challenge. *When I was promoted to sales and marketing director for Region 5, we were the lowest performing region of the thirty regional territories. My challenge was to bring the sales and overall performance numbers up as quickly as possible.*

Action. *To do so, I met with the twenty-person sales staff, jointly established some aggressive goals for the next six to twelve months, and developed a promotional strategy to increase customer awareness of our products which included incentives for new purchases within a stated length of time.*

Result. *Within ninety days, sales were up by 15 percent, and by year-end we were second in the nation with $1.2 million in sales*

Now, write your Life Experience Stories on a separate sheet or on your computer, for each position. You should have at least eight to ten stories in all. If you wish, you can use the terms in Authentic Retirement Worksheet 4 to help trigger ideas for stories.

Story 1.

Story 2.

Story 3.

Story 4.

Story 6.

Story 7.

Story 8.

Story 9.

Story 10.

Do you notice any themes in your stories? Write them here:

8. Authentic Retirement Worksheet No. 6: Desired Activities

You are now ready to explore the sixth element of your Authentic Retirement, Desired Activities for your retirement lifestyle.

Please respond to each question below. If an important activity or element of your desired retirement lifestyle is not listed, write it in at the end.

1. Will you work? _____ yes; _____ no
If you will work, will it be:

   _____full-time
   _____part-time
   _____contract
   _____temporary
   _____bridge/project employment
   _____entrepreneurship
   _____phased retirement
   _____other

How many hours or days per week?

2. Will you spend more time at hobbies? _____ yes; _____ no
Which ones and how?

3. Will you give back to the community, with your money or time? _____ yes; _____ no
If so, through what organization or means?

How much time will you spend doing this each week or month?

4. Will you spend more time with children, grandchildren, foster kids, animals, parents, or…? _____ yes; _____ no
   How would you like that to look (what activities, how much time, etc.)?

5. Will you spend more or less time with your spouse? _____ more; _____ less
Will that change your relationship? _____ yes; _____ no
How?

Coaching Authentic Retirement 159

6. Will you spend time managing retirement accounts or investments?
   _____ yes; _____ no
   How would you like that to look?

7. Will you get more involved in your church or spiritual development?
   _____ yes; _____ no
   How would you like that to look?

8. Will you get more involved in political activities? _____ yes; _____ no
   How would you like that to look?

9. Will you incorporate more personal time to just "be" (versus "doing" something all the time)? _____ yes; _____ no
   How would you like that to look?

10. Will you increase the time spent in leisure, exercise and recreation?
    _____ yes; _____ no
    How would you like that to look?

11. Do you want to travel in retirement? _____ yes; _____ no
    To what locations?

    How frequently?

12. Will you go back to school, take classes, or otherwise enhance your learning? _____ yes; _____ no

   Which ones? What would you love to learn?

13. Do you want to contribute some of your knowledge through teaching, consulting, or mentoring? _____yes; _____ no

   How would you like that to be?

14. Would you like to pursue a "work substitute" through volunteering, being a docent at a museum, or doing service for the community? _____yes; _____ no
   How would you like that to be?

15. What kinds of entertainment would you like to integrate into your retirement?

16. Other?

9. Authentic Retirement Worksheet No. 7: Environment

You are now ready to explore the seventh factor of your Authentic Retirement, Environment. Your environment can either enhance or detract from your enjoyment of your retirement life. The items listed below will help you evaluate each aspect of your environment so that you can design it just the way you want.

1. Geographical Location. Where would you like to live? In the state and city where you live -- or somewhere else altogether? Perhaps this is a perfect time to explore that option realistically. If you will work, would you like to work in an office or outdoors? In an urban or rural setting? Perhaps have a home-based business?

My ideal location is: _____.

2. Pace. A second aspect of your environment is the pace of your retirement lifestyle. Do you enjoy an environment that is bustling and busy, or do you prefer a peaceful, slower pace? Would your ideal retirement pace be slower or faster than when you were working?

My ideal pace is: _____.

3. Support. The degree of support you have is also important. One way to avoid either stress or boredom, depending on your personal tendencies, is to surround yourself with a supportive environment -- one in which you have a sense of significance, autonomy, challenge and support, and in which there are relatively few unmodifiable stresses. You may need to create this if it is not yet a part of your life!

I prefer to have: ___ little support; ___ moderate support; ___ a lot of support.

4. Income. How much money will you need to finance your retirement lifestyle? When we get to Worksheet 8, you will determine whether or not you can afford this lifestyle with your current assets.

My ideal retirement income is $_____ per _____.

My anticipated retirement income is $_____ per _____.

5. Focus of Activities. It is also important to evaluate whether you prefer to do most of your activities alone, with one or two close friends or family, or with a lot of people most of the time. To help you evaluate your optimal focus, consider the following profiles of the soloist, the partner, and the team personality.

Soloist Profile

- is independent
- prefers being and working alone; likes privacy
- is highly creative and contemplative
- has a few carefully chosen friends
- resists authority
- is motivated by opportunity to create and to get credit for creation
- likes to take risks
- biggest fear: loss of control

Partner Profile

- enjoys (and needs) give and take feedback when making decisions and in conversation
- is most creative in context of a close relationship
- has a few long-term friends
- needs equal amounts of time alone and with others
- is excellent listener
- feels power comes from shared resources
- shares risk-taking with partner
- biggest fear: rejection by partner

Team Personality Profile

- enjoys *esprit de corps* of large group of friends, whether in social or work or volunteer setting, including process of gaining consensus
- wants to be alone about 20 percent of the time
- is motivated by competition
- forms many friendships easily
- comfortable with authority figures
- is most creative in context of praise from team members and from leader
- enjoys belonging to clubs
- shares risks with team members and leader
- biggest fear: loneliness

You may find you have aspects of two of these profiles, or maybe even all three --but you probably have more qualities from one than any of the others. Which one most closely describes you:

___ soloist
___ partner
___ team personality

6. Primary Function. Next, consider your activities. Do you prefer to work/play primarily with people, with data, or with things? Think about your hobbies and past jobs. What activities have given you the most joy: those involving interaction with people, working with data or information, or working on things with your hands?

I prefer to be involved primarily in activities involving:

   ___   people
   ___   data
   ___   things

To summarize: What would your ideal day in retirement be like? Where would you be? What other aspects of environment are important to you? Write your thoughts - a vision of your ideal retirement – below, considering what you have discovered in worksheets 1 through 7.

10. *Authentic Retirement Worksheet No. 8: The Finance Factor*

Now that you have explored your life's purpose and the other six factors of your Authentic Retirement, you should have a clearer picture of your desired lifestyle. Now, you will evaluate your financial needs and resources to ensure that you can afford your retirement. We save this aspect of your planning for last, because we want you to clarify your dreams, goals and ideals before factoring in money.

The following worksheet can help, but may be overly simplistic For more accurate results, see your financial planner and/or one of the following financial calculator programs:
http://sites.stockpoint.com/aarp_rc/wm/Retirement/Retirement.asp?act=LOGIN
http://www.nylim.com/rcg/0,2058,70_1013274,00.html
http://www.womenswallstreet.com/WWS/Calculators.aspx?titleid=99
http://www.principal.com/calculators/retire.htm

INCOME

1. Current retirement savings/assets: $_____

2. Amount I will save by retirement: $_____

3. Subtotal: $_____

4. Growth/return on investment: _____%

5. 3 x 4 $_____

6. Total 3 + 5 $_____

Less:

Inflation (4%) x item 3 $_____

Subtotal $_____

Plus Social Security benefits $_____
(see http://www.ssa.gov/planners/calculators.htm)

Other income at retirement (rental income,
royalties, pension, wage/salary, etc.) $_____

TOTAL INCOME $_____

EXPENSES

List your retirement expenses on a separate
sheet,, including taxes owed; write total
monthly expenses here: $_____

How many years will you be retired?   x _____
TOTAL EXPENSE REQUIREMENTS $_____

Subtract Total Expenses from Total Income: $_____

Is the number positive or negative? If positive, you probably have adequate income for your retirement. If negative, you will either need to:

     a. work longer before retiring and accumulate additional money
     b. reduce projected retirement expenses
     c. find a way to increase retirement assets through income-generating investments or other means
     d. plan to work part-time in retirement

What is your strategy for making up any shortfall?

11. My Beliefs About Money

This worksheet is designed to explore your beliefs about money, and how they may affect your retirement. Complete each of the six steps below.

1. What were you taught about money by your parents and other influential people in childhood?

Example: Money doesn't grow on trees!

2. What beliefs support those beliefs? What are their implications?

Example: If one believes there isn't enough money, it will tend to be a self-fulfilling prophecy: they unconsciously won't allow themselves to have enough and will struggle to make ends meet; even if they have enough they won't spend it

3. Which of those beliefs continue to serve you now?

As we grow, we must re-examine the beliefs we were taught early on and which are now largely unconscious. If they still serve us, we can then consciously choose to include them in our current beliefs; if they don't, we can replace them with beliefs that serve us better now.

4. Which beliefs would you like to eliminate and replace with alternate beliefs?

Example: if you were taught that money was not to be talked about, or have a low deservingness level, you may find yourself discounting your fees, giving services away, etc.

5. What new beliefs would you like to hold about money instead of those that no longer serve you?

6. Is there anything standing in the way of your beginning to transform your beliefs about money now?

Finally, in the space below, write a Statement of Abundance which incorporates all of your desired beliefs about money and your vision for your Authentic Retirement. Plan to review it daily.

MY STATEMENT OF ABUNDANCE

---

12. Coper/Thriver Quiz

How do you deal with transitions? On a scale of 1 to 3, rate the following statements putting the score in the ODD column for the odd-numbered statements and the score in the EVEN column for the even-numbered statements.

    1 = NOT TRUE of me at all
    2 = SOMETIMES true of me
    3 = FREQUENTLY true of me

STATEMENT	ODD	EVEN
1. I often suspect the motives behind other people's acts and decisions.		
2. I know myself well, including my strengths and weaknesses, beliefs, values, and priorities.		
3. I am a loner, and have very few friends.		
4. I believe in a Power greater than myself, or regularly practice a religion.		
5. I haven't thought much about my purpose in life.		
6. I choose how I will feel about my circumstances, rather than letting them determine my mood.		
7. I find it most effective to expect the worst so that I'm not disappointed.		
8. I have a strong network of family, friends, and professionals from which I draw support.		
9. I know how to manipulate people and circumstances to get them to do what I want.		
10. I am not afraid to feel my whole range of emotions, whether comfortable or not.		

STATEMENT	ODD	EVEN
11. In my list of priorities in life, work and/or financial status is higher than my family.		
12. I take good care of myself, including eating a healthy diet, exercising regularly, monitoring my stress level, and getting enough sleep.		
13. Spirituality is not an important part of my life.		
14. I enjoy taking risks -- and regularly do so.		
15. I rarely feel angry, depressed, frustrated, or sad.		
16. I organize my life around a strong sense of purpose, and actively initiate necessary changes and set ambitious goals to carry out my purpose as I understand it.		
17. I believe that most things are either right or wrong, good or bad -- no in between.		
18. Before I act on a choice I make, I think about the ramifications of my actions on other people and on other parts of my life.		
19. The things that have happened to me are usually someone else's fault.		
20. I am able to bounce back when things don't go my way, and to trust that eventually I will come out of the situation a better person.		
21. The people I spend time with often complain and gossip about others.		
22. I am not bothered by uncertain or ambiguous times in my life; I use them to		

STATEMENT	ODD	EVEN
grow.		
23. I often work evenings and weekends, and rarely take vacations.		
24. I actively seek out new experiences, and am committed to ongoing personal growth.		
25. If the weather doesn't fit my plans, I often become depressed.		
26. I believe I can do anything that I put my mind to.		
TOTAL	Coper	Thriver

Now, add your total score from the ODD column; this is your "Coper Quotient." Next, add your total score from the EVEN column; this is your "Thriver Quotient."

If your score is between 26 and 39 on either column, you have a strong tendency toward that approach to transition. If you have a low Coper Quotient, you will normally have a high Thriver Quotient. If you are equally balanced between both, you find yourself engaging in ineffective strategies in approaching change more often than you need to in today's constantly changing world.

13. Coaching Questions For Each Thriver Trait Cluster

Attentiveness:
- What do you need to be [more] aware of now?
- What is your growing edge here?
- Who/what is driving your actions and/or thoughts?
- What new experience(s) could you embrace that might help you?

Groundedness:
- What do your spiritual practices/beliefs tell you? How could they ground you now?
- Who do you have in your support system that you could turn to now? Who else do you need?
- What will it take for you to bounce back from this?

Trust:
- What are you feeling now? What else? Are you overlooking or suppressing any of your feelings? If they could speak, what would they say?
- What is ambiguous? What temporary structures can you erect in your life during this phase?
- Who/what do you trust in your experience? Who/what do you distrust? What would need to happen for you to trust more? What do you need to let go of? Will you?
- How can you nurture yourself?

Proactive Purpose:
- What do you believe your life purpose is? [Refer to Authentic Retirement Worksheet 1.] How can it guide you now? If it had a voice, what would it say? How does each option serve/express your life purpose? How does it not?
- What is your biggest dream/the best outcome you can imagine here?
- What do you need to fulfill your vision? What is your first step?

Optimistic Confidence:
- How is your self-confidence being enhanced now? What will it take to build it more?
- What past experience can you draw on? Has there been a time when you successfully navigated a similar transition?
- What risks are you being called to make now? What are the potential consequences/what would happen if you took them? What needs to happen to move forward?
- How could you look at this differently? What other labels/terms could you use?
- How could you be more flexible?

- How could you have more fun with this?
- What is the positive side of the situation?

Systems Thinking:
- How will this decision affect other people in your life? Other aspects of your life?
- How could you view your options more objectively?
- What's funny in this situation? What would it take for you to laugh at yourself?
- What does balance look/feel like to you? How can you create it?

14. Should I Work In Retirement?

A number of factors will affect your decision as to whether or not to continue working (full-time or something less than that) during retirement. The following quiz will help you decide.

Question	Yes	Not Applicable	No
1. Do I need additional income to satisfy my financial needs?			
2. Would I like additional income to fulfill some of my financial wants?			
3. Is it important for me to feel like I am making a contribution through your efforts?			
4. Do I need company-provided health insurance or other benefits?			
5. Am I healthy enough to withstand the demands of work?			
6. Do I need the social companionship of working with others?			
7. Am I an achievement-oriented person?			
8. Do I feel rewarded by helping others?			
9. Do I have an unfulfilled dream that can now be fulfilled through work?			
10. Do I need or desire to be physically active through work?			
11. Is it important to me to do something productive or useful with my life?			
12. Am I comfortable having a work schedule and structure?			
TOTAL			

15. Is Entrepreneurship Right For You?

Are you thinking of starting your own business? If so, please indicate "yes" or "no" for each of the following questions to see if entrepreneurship is a suitable option for you.

	Question	Yes	No
1	Is it important to you to accomplish something meaningful with your life?		
2	Do you typically set both short- and long-term goals for yourself?		
3	Do you usually achieve your goals?		
4	Do you enjoy working on your own?		
5	Do you like to perform a variety of tasks in your job?		
6	Are you self-disciplined?		
7	Do you like to be in control of your working environment?		
8	Do you take full responsibility for your successes *and* failures?		
9	Can you place the needs of your business above your family when necessary?		
10	Are you in excellent physical, mental and emotional health?		
11	Do you have the drive and energy to create a successful business?		
12	Do you have a basic knowledge of the subject matter in which you will be doing business?		
13	Have you ever been so engrossed in your work that time passed unnoticed?		
14	Do you consider "failures" as opportunities to learn and grow?		
15	Can you hold to your ideas and goals even when others disagree with you?		
16	Are you willing to take moderate risks to achieve your goals?		
17	Can you afford to lose the money you invest in your business?		
18	When the need arises, are you willing to do a job that may not interest you?		
19	Are you willing to work hard to acquire new skills?		
20	Do you usually stick with a project until it is completed?		
	TOTAL:		

Evaluating Your Answers:

17-20 "yes"   Entrepreneurship is for you!
14-17 "yes"   You may be suited to entrepreneurship
10-14 "yes"   Work within a team or organization may be a better fit than self-employment
5-10 "yes"   Carefully examine your choice to be sure owning a business is what you want to do!
0-5 "yes"   Entrepreneurship is probably *not* your best career choice

16. My Retirement Health

Did you know that a significant factor in your level of health in retirement is due to personal choices? Motivational speaker Brian Tracy has stated that (paraphrasing here) our experience today is the result of our cumulative behaviors and thoughts from yesterday. Please respond to the questions below to begin creating your vision of health.

1. Do you think of yourself as healthy? ____ yes; ____ no

2. Do you perceive yourself to be more or less healthy than you used to be? ____ yes; ____ no (if you answered yes, skip to question 5; otherwise go to question 3)

3. If you responded no to questions 1 or 2, what are the major contributing factors to your lack of health? List them below.

4. Reviewing the reasons/barriers you listed in question 3, which of them are unchangeable? Which could be changed? For example, just because you come from a family that has a history of heart disease does not necessarily mean that you will have that disease if you engage in preventive health practices. Put a "C" next to the changeable ones and a "U" next to the unchangeable ones (e.g., paralysis from an accident) in your answers to question 3.

5. Now, imagine that you are as healthy as you would like to be, whether you currently feel that way or have a ways to go. In the space below, describe how you feel as though you were experiencing it now. What physical sensation does it give you? What does it allow you to do? What do you no longer have to do (e.g., depend on others to take care of you)? How do you move your body or enjoy healthy food so that it feels good to you? Write your Vision of Health below.

MY VISION OF HEALTH

6. To achieve your vision, you will need to stay motivated. Name all of the reasons you can think of that you would like to maintain or improve your health according to your vision (which fuel that motivation) below:

7. Next, state the action steps that you will take in the next (a) week, (b) month, and (c) year to improve your health.

Weekly action:

Monthly action:

Annual action:

8. Congratulations! You are well on your way to better health. Along with regular check-ups, good diet, regular exercise, sufficient sleep, and abstaining from unhealthy habits, you will achieve your goals. The space below is for you to monitor your progress over the coming weeks.

PROGRESS TOWARD MY HEALTH GOALS

Question	Yes	No
Did I stick to my desired diet?		
Did I exercise at least 5 times per week?		
Did I get enough sleep for me nearly every night?		
Did I abstain from drugs and tobacco?		
Did I avoid excessive alcohol?		
[List your goals below and respond accordingly)		

17. Top Ten Indicators To Refer To A Mental Health Professional

Following are guidelines to help coaches determine whether and when to refer a client to a therapist or other mental health professional.

Your client:

1. **Is exhibiting a decline in his/her ability to experience pleasure and/or an increase in being sad, hopeless and helpless**
    - As a coach you may notice that your client is not as upbeat as usual.
    - He/she may talk much more frequently about how awful life/the world is and that nothing can be done about it.
    - The client may make comments about "why bother" or "what's the use"
    - There will be a decline in talking about things that are enjoyable.
    - He/she may stop doing things they like to do (examples: going to the movies, visiting with friends, participating in athletic events or being a spectator of sporting events)
    - The client begins to talk about being unable to do anything that forwards their dreams or desires

2. **Has intrusive thoughts or is unable to concentrate or focus**
    - As a coach you may notice that your client is not able to focus on their goals or the topic of conversation.
    - The client is unable to complete their action steps and isn't aware of what got in the way.
    - You notice that your client begins talking about unpleasant events during the course of talking about themselves and their goals.
    - The client tells you that unpleasant thoughts keep popping into their minds at inopportune moments or when they are thinking about or doing other things and that they can't seem to get away from these thoughts.
    - Your client tells you about recurring scary dreams that they didn't have before.
    - Your client reports that they have so many thoughts swirling in their heads and that they can't get them to slow down.

3. **Is unable to get to sleep or awakens during the night and is unable to get back to sleep or sleeps excessively**
    - Your client comes to their coaching sessions tired and exhausted.
    - Your client begins talking about not being able to get to sleep or how he/she just wants to sleep all the time.
    - Your client may report to you how he/she gets to sleep and then wakes up and can't get back to sleep.
    - Your client tells you how they need to take naps during the day, something they have not done before.
    - Your client reports that they fell asleep at an inopportune time or place.

4. **Has a change in appetite: decrease in appetite or increase in appetite**
    - Your client reports that he/she isn't hungry and just doesn't want to eat.
    - Your client reports that he/she is eating all the time, usually sweets or junk food, whether or not they are hungry.
    - Your client says they don't get any enjoyment from eating when they did in the past.
    - Your client reports that they are not sitting down to eat with friends or family when they did in the past.

5. **Is feeling guilty because others have suffered or died**
    - Your client reports that they feel guilty because they are alive or have not been injured.
    - Your client states that they don't understand why they are still here/alive when others have had to suffer/die
    - Your client doesn't want to move forward with their goals because they don't deserve to have the life they choose, especially when other people have had to suffer/die.
    - Your client questions their right to have a fulfilling life/career in the face of all that has happened
    - Your client expresses the belief that he/she is unworthy of having a satisfying life.

6. **Has feelings of despair or hopelessness**
    - According to your client nothing in life is OK.
    - Your client misses session times or says they want to quit coaching because life is not worth living or they don't deserve to get what they want.
    - Your client moves into excessive negative thinking.
    - Your client says that they can't make a difference or that whatever they do doesn't matter.
    - Your client has the attitude of "Why bother?"

7. **Is being hyper alert and/or excessively tired**
    - Your client reports that they can't relax.
    - Your client states that they are jumping at the slightest noise.
    - Your client reports that it feels like they always have to be on guard.
    - Your client states that they are listening for any little sound that is out of the ordinary.
    - Your client reports that they have no energy.
    - Your client states that they can't do their usual chores because they are so tired.
    - Your client states that it takes too much energy to do things they normally did in the past.

8. **Has increased irritability or outbursts of anger**

- Your client becomes increasingly belligerent or argumentative with you or other people.
- Your client reports that everyone or everything annoys them.
- Your client starts making comments about how miserable everyone and everything is.
- Your client reports that other people in their life are telling them how miserable/angry they have become.
- Your client reports getting into arguments with people.
- Your client states that they get so upset they don't know what to do with themselves.
- Your client reports that they feel like a "pressure cooker" or are "ready to burst."
- Your client increasingly tells you about wanting to do or doing things that would harm themselves or others (examples: wanting to put their fist through a window; wanting to punch someone; wanting to hit someone/something with their car).

9. **Has impulsive and risk-taking behavior**
    - Your client reports doing things, such as going on a buying spree, without thinking about the consequences of their behavior.
    - Your client tells you that something came to their mind so they went and did it without thinking about the outcome.
    - Your client reports an increase in doing things that could be detrimental to themselves or others (examples: increase in promiscuous sexual behavior; increase in alcohol/drug consumption; deciding to get married after knowing someone an unusually short period of time).

10. **Has thoughts of death and/or suicide**
    - Your client begins talking a lot about death, not just a fear of dying.
    - Your client alludes to the fact that dying would be appropriate for them.
    - Your client makes comments that to die right now would be OK with them.
    - Your client becomes fascinated with what dying would be like.
    - Your client talks about ways to die.
    - Your client talks about going to a better place and how wonderful it would be and seems to be carried away by the thought.
    - Your client tells you they know how they would kill themselves if they wanted to/had the chance.
    - Your client alludes to having a plan or way they would die/go to a better place/leave the planet/leave the situation/get out of here.
    - Whereas previously your client was engaging, personable and warm and now they present to you as cold, distant and aloof tell them what you are observing and ask them what has changed for them. This is often a signal that they have disengaged from living and are silently thinking or planning to suicide.
    - Some questions you might ask your client if you are unclear about what is going on with them or their intentions: "Are you wanting to die?" "How

would you die if you decided to?" "Are you planning on dieing?" "When are you planning on dieing?"
- If you have any inclination or indication that your client is planning on dying/committing suicide immediately refer them to an emergency room or call 911.
    1. Tell your client that you care about them, are concerned for them, that you are taking what they say seriously and that they must get help immediately.
    2. If the client balks at what you are saying, gets belligerent or even more distant AND you become even more concerned about them, you may need to tell them you will break confidentiality because of your concern for their well-being and that you will call 911 (You can call your local 911 and give them the address and phone number of your client, even if it is in another state, and they can contact the client's local 911 dispatcher).

If is important to note that the appearance of any one of these indicators, except for #10 which must be referred and followed up on immediately, does not indicate the immediate need for a referral to a psychotherapist or community mental health agency; everyone can experience a very brief episode of any of the indicators. However, if you see that several indicators are emerging and that the client is not presenting as whole, competent and capable then it is time for a referral to a mental health professional.

Prepared by: Lynn F. Meinke, MA, RN, CLC, CSLC
               Life Coach
               Chair: Life-Personal Coach Committee of ICF

18. My Social Network

Below, please list your friends, family members, and other relationships with people who comprise part of your social network currently (pre-retirement):

Close/intimate friends and family	Change in retirement? Yes No	Work-related friends	Change in retirement? Yes No	Acquaintances/ connected by a hobby, church, or other venue.	Change in retirement? Yes No

Based on the inventory above, what kinds of relationships do you need to cultivate to round out your social network for retirement:

_____ close/intimate
_____ church-related

_____ work-related
_____ connected to a hobby
_____ share an interest
_____ other:

Where will you go/what will you do to cultivate these relationships?

19. What Will I Do With My Time?

One of the rewards you have earned as you retire is the opportunity to spend more time doing what you want to do: pursuing hobbies, seeing friends and family, traveling, cooking, gardening, golfing, or whatever else suits your fancy. But many retirees find themselves feeling stuck, busier than ever with the day-to-day tasks of life, and unable to optimize their leisure time. This exercise is designed to help you develop greater awareness of how you actually spend your time now (including what activities are "wasting" time or keeping you from what you would like to do). Then, you can better envision and define what you want to be different, and an action plan to achieve that desired state.

Step 1. Keep a time log. For a period of one week (or more if you can!), on a spiral notebook or other tablet that is easy to keep with you throughout the day, record *everything* you do from awakening to going to bed. From grooming to checking email, working (and what you do while at work) to exercise, time with your spouse to a call to your grandchild – write it down including the minute you start each activity (that way the next activity's starting time becomes the prior activity's ending time). Leave about two inches of space at the right hand side of your log. Here's an example:

Date: _____

Time	Activity
6:30	Got up, brushed teeth, washed face, got dressed
6:50	Made coffee, read paper
7:15	Went for a walk
8:00	Ate breakfast
8:30	Showered and dressed
9:00	Drove to grocery store

Step 2: Analyze activities. Now that you have your log of at least seven days' activities, it is time to see where the time went! Add two columns to the right of your log (in the 2 inches you left at the right). Check the appropriate column as to whether the activity was time well spent or a time waster (note that on some you may check both columns if you wanted to do that activity but spent too long at it, as with surfing the Internet and getting sidetracked). When you are finished with this analysis, total the time well spent each day and the time wasted each day.

Time	Activity	Time Well Spent	Time Waster
6:30	Got up, brushed teeth, washed face, got dressed		
6:50	Made coffee, read paper		
7:15	Went for a walk		
8:00	Ate breakfast		
8:30	Showered and dressed		
9:00	Drove to grocery store		
	TOTALS		

Step 3: Graph your time log. Now, using a pie chart like that illustrated below, please indicate the percentages of time you spend on each category of activities, using the data in your log. Categories can include:

- Work
- Spouse time
- Family time
- Time with friends
- Hobby
- Recreation
- Exercise
- Personal grooming
- Eating
- Paperwork

and any other categories relevant to you.

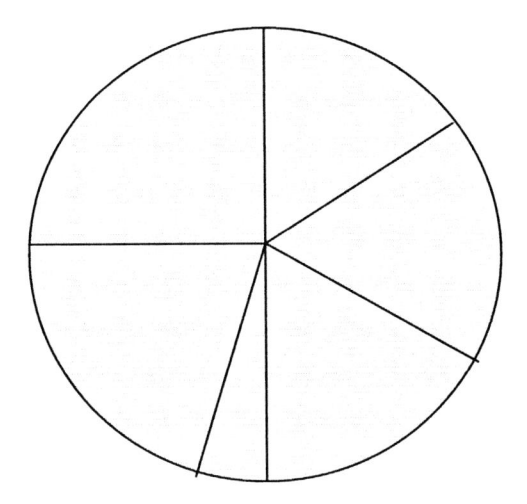

What can you conclude from the exercise so far? Write your conclusions and discoveries below (e.g., "I'm spending too much time looking for things – need to get more organized."):

Step 4: Draw your desired graph. Now, using a pie chart like that illustrated above, please indicate the percentages of time you *would like to spend* on each category of activities that is important to you.

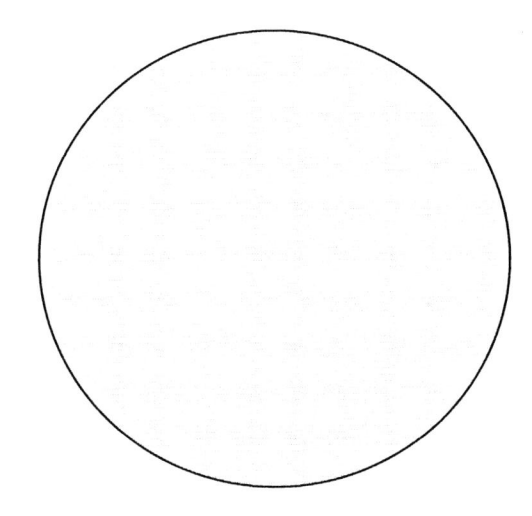

Step 5. Develop an action plan. Finally, develop a series of action steps that will help you transform your current time allocation to the desired one, and set a goal for when that will be accomplished.

Action Steps:	Goal or Timeline
1.	
2.	
3.	
4.	
5.	
6.	
7.	
8.	
9.	
10.	

20. Retirement Satisfaction Inventory

As published in "Assessing Retirement Satisfaction and Perceptions of Retirement Experiences," by Frank J. Floyd et al, *Psychology and Aging* (Copyright ©1992 by the American Psychological Association; Reprinted with permission)

Please answer the following questions as carefully as possible. You may choose not to answer some questions, but you are encouraged to answer as many as possible.

1. Before retirement, how gratifying did you find your job compared to other areas of your life

1	2	3	4	5	6
very gratifying	ungratifying	somewhat ungratifying	somewhat gratifying	gratifying	very gratifying

2. Before retirement, how satisfied were you with your job?

1	2	3	4	5	6
very dissatisfied	dissatisfied	somewhat dissatisfied	somewhat satisfied	satisfied	very satisfied

3. Before retirement, how satisfied did you expect to be with retirement?

| 1 | 2 | 3 | 4 | 5 | 6 |

How important were each of the following in your decision to retire? (If a question does not apply, mark unimportant)

4. I reached mandatory retirement age.

1	2	3	4	5	6
very unimportant	unimportant	somewhat unimportant	somewhat important	important	very important

5. I was in poor health
   1   2   3   4   5   6

6. My spouse was in poor health.
   1   2   3   4   5   6

7. I could finally afford it.
   1   2   3   4   5   6

8. I was laid off, fired or my hours were cut back.
   1   2   3   4   5   6

9. I was experiencing difficulties with people at work.
   1   2   3   4   5   6

10. I was pressured to retire by employer.
    1   2   3   4   5   6

1	2	3	4	5	6
very unimportant	unimportant	somewhat unimportant	somewhat important	important	very important

11. I was offered incentives to retire by my company.
    1   2   3   4   5   6

12. I wanted to spend more time with my family.
    1   2   3   4   5   6

13. I wanted more time to pursue my interests (such as hobbies and travel).
    1   2   3   4   5   6

14. I wanted to make room for younger people.
    1   2   3   4   5   6

15. I disliked my job.
    1   2   3   4   5   6

16. I experienced too much stress at work.
    1   2   3   4   5   6

17. I had difficulty handling the physical demands of my job.
    1   2   3   4   5   6

18. My spouse wanted me to retire.
    1   2   3   4   5   6

19. Other considerations (please explain)
_____

_____

Please indicate your current level of satisfaction with the following areas of your life?

20. My Marriage

0	1	2	3	4	5	6
N/A	very dissatisfied	dissatisfied	somewhat dissatisfied	somewhat satisfied	satisfied	very satisfied

21. My financial situation
    1   2   3   4   5   6

22. My physical health
    1   2   3   4   5   6

23. The health of my spouse
    1   2   3   4   5   6

24. The quality of my residence
    1   2   3   4   5   6

25. Relationships with other family members (such as children, brothers, sisters, cousins, nieces and nephews)
    1   2   3   4   5   6

26. My level of physical activity
    1   2   3   4   5   6

27. My access to transportation
    1   2   3   4   5   6

28. Services from community agencies and programs
    1   2   3   4   5   6

29. Services from government aid programs (such as Social Security, Medicare, subsidized housing, nutrition programs, etc.)
    1   2   3   4   5   6

30. My personal safety
    1   2   3   4   5   6

31. After retirement, how easy or difficult were the first few months?
    1   2   3   4   5   6
    very, very   difficult   somewhat   somewhat   easy   very
    difficult   difficult   easy   easy

32. Overall, how does your life since retirement compare with your life before retirement?
    1   2   3   4   5   6
    much   worse   somewhat   somewhat   better   much
    worse   worse   better   better

33. How often do you participate in leisure activities with friends?
    1   2   3   4
    never   seldom   sometimes   often

34. How often do you participate in leisure activities with family?
    1   2   3   4
    never   seldom   sometimes   often

35. How often do you participate in physical activities (such as dancing, bicycling or walking)?
    1   2   3   4

How important is each of the following in making your retirement enjoyable?

36. Freedom to pursue my own interests
    1   2   3   4
    unimportant   slightly   moderately   very
                      unimportant   important   important

1	2	3	4
unimportant	slightly unimportant	moderately important	very important

37. Not having to work
    1   2   3   4

38. Spending more time with my family
    1   2   3   4

39. Spending more time with my friends
    1   2   3   4

40. More control over my own life
    1   2   3   4

41. No boss
    1   2   3   4

42. More travel
    1   2   3   4

43. Less stress
    1   2   3   4

44. Being with a group of other retired persons
    1   2   3   4

45. More time for activities
    1   2   3   4

46. Participation in volunteer organizations
    1   2   3   4

47. Being carefree
    1   2   3   4

48. More time to think
    1   2   3   4

49. More relaxed
    1   2   3   4

50. Can be alone more
    1   2   3   4

51. Overall, how satisfied are you with your retirement right now?

1	2	3	4	5	6
very dissatisfied	dissatisfied	somewhat dissatisfied	somewhat satisfied	satisfied	very satisfied

21. Retirement Lifestyle Template™

Item	True (T) or False (F)	Activities that currently fulfill	New activities or people that could fulfill
Authentic Retirement Criteria			
I have clarified my life purpose			
I know my key values			
I have identified what motivates me and my interests			
I know my talents			
I have clarified what aspects of my past experience I want to draw from			
I have thought through my desired retirement activities			
I know what my ideal retirement environment and lifestyle will involve			
I have analyzed my finances and determined my savings, investment, income and expense requirements			
Financial Factors			
I have adequate financial reserves to retire and generate the income I need			
If I don't have the reserves I need, I have planned to work or otherwise make up the deficit			
I have determined how to meet my expense requirements in retirement			

I have invested my money in ways that are comfortable to me in risk and reward			
Lifestyle Aspects			
I have evaluated my desired place(s) of residence in retirement and decided what is best for me.			
[If applicable] I have begun preparing to move to my desired retirement home.			
I have identified ways to continue learning in retirement, whether by formal education or less formal means.			
Emotional Factors			
I have an optimistic attitude toward retiring			
I am a "Thriver" (not a Coper) in dealing with transitions			
I have faced and overcome any fears I had about retirement			
I know how to prevent boredom in retirement			
I have developed a concept of God and have a vibrant spiritual life.			
Work Issues			
I know whether or not I will work in retirement			
If I will work, I have clarified my desired hours and type of work and know how to find it			
If I will not work, I have arranged a work substitute to ensure satisfaction of my key motivators in retirement			

Identity Issues			
I have thought through the ways my identity will change in retirement			
I am comfortable with my identity without work			
I am less concerned about what other people think of me, and more willing to be authentic, now that I am retiring			
I am willing to self-disclose to become more authentic			
Health and Aging			
I have a positive attitude about getting older			
I willingly embrace the idea that my retirement years are designed to reveal new parts of me			
I have defined for myself what it means to age			
I exercise regularly			
I eat a healthy diet			
I minimize stress			
I get adequate sleep			
I nurture my body, mind and spirit to contribute to greater health			
I have arranged health insurance for retirement			
I have purchased long-term care insurance for myself			
Social/Relationship Shifts			
My spouse or partner and I have discussed possible changes to our relationship and lifestyle resulting from retirement			
I have a number of friends who are non-work related			

If I have grandchildren to raise or parents to care for, I have accepted that responsibility and incorporated it into my retirement planning			
I have considered how my family and friends will respond to my retirement, and know how to address their concerns.			
Leisure and Travel			
I know how much of my retirement lifestyle I want to spend doing leisure activities and hobbies.			
I have several activities or hobbies I like to do that do not involve work			
I have decided how much and how often I want to travel in retirement			
I have examined my motives for retirement and determined that my reasons for traveling are appropriate (i.e. I'm not trying to escape)			
I have taken one or more retirement assessments to ensure that my retirement transition timing is right and/or to enhance my understanding of my motivators and personality			

22. My Retirement Lifestyle Profile

Name: _____

Summary of my desired lifestyle:

Proposed retirement date:

Purpose fulfilled:

Values actualized:

Motivators met:

Talents used:

Experience drawn upon:

Desired activities to be pursued:

Environment/lifestyle:

Financial status:

Anticipated barriers, if any:

How barriers will be overcome:

23. Marketing Priorities Checklist

Indicate for each of the categories listed the anticipated cost and time it would take (low, medium or high), the potential impact it could have, whether it is a short or long time horizon, and your decision as to whether to use it in your marketing plan. For those you will use, number them in order of priority in the righthand column.

Category	Resource Usage (cost and time)			Potential Impact			Time Horizon		Use?		If yes, Order of Priority
	L	M	H	L	M	H	S	L	Y	N	#
Telephone											
Toll-Free #											
Answering Service											
Telemarketing											
Teleclass											
Interview Show/Call											
Yellow pages ad											
Radio											
Spot											
Sponsor											
Call-In Show											
Television											
Spot											
Sponsor											
Advertorial											
Cable show											
Internet											
Ezine											
Discussion List											
Banner Ad											
Affiliate Program											
Discussion Lists											
Target Emailing											
Web page											
Website											
Co-op Ad											
Articles											
Search engine placement											

Newspaper										
Classified Ad										
Display Ad										
Press Release										
Feature Article										
Column										
Authoring										
Articles										
Columns										
Surveys										
White Papers										
Newsletter/Ezine										
Press Kit										
Introduction letter										
Press Releases										
Biography										
Fact Sheet										
Published Articles										
Company Literature										
Business Card										
Speaking										
Clubs										
Associations										
Keynote										
Seminars										
Training										
Teleclass										
Networking										
Market group 1										
Market group 2										
Market group 3										
Conferences										
Exhibit										
Speak										
Volunteer										
Sponsor										

Books										
Ebook										
Trade paperback										
Co-Author										
Contributor										
Tapes										
CD's										
Internet-based program or product										
Networking Event/Meeting										
Sponsor										
Speak										
Participate										
Coaching										
Free session										
Demo										
Other										
Direct Mail										
Other										

24. Resources for Retirement Coaches

BOOKS

Angowski, Rogak, Lisa, *Time Off From Work* (Wiley 1994)

Bench, Marcia, *Discover Your Niche: With the Gems System*, (High Flight Press 2003)

Bench, Marcia, *Fill Your Practice: Building Your Marketing Machine*, (High Flight Press 2003)

Bench, Marcia, *Launch Your Practice: Start-Up from A to Z,* (High Flight Press 2003)

Bland, Warren, *Retire In Style: 50 Affordable Places Across America*, (Next Decade Inc 2002)

Butterworth, Eric, *Spiritual Economics* (Unity House 2001)

Cohen, Dian, *The New Retirement*, (Doubleday, 1999)

Dlugozima, Hope et al, *Six Months Off* (Holt 1996)

Dychtwald, Ken, *Age Wave*, (Tarcher 1988)

Finley, Mike, *Finding Work After 50* (Brownherron, 2002)

Freedman, Marc, *Prime Time: How Baby-Boomers Will revolutionize Retirement and Transform America* (Public Affairs, 2002)

Fyock, Catherine, Dorton, *Unretirement: A Career Guide for the Retired..the Soon-To-Be-Retired….the Never-Want-To-Be-Retired*, (AMA, 1994)

Goldberg, Beverly, *Age Works: What Corporate America Must Do to Survive the Graying of the Workforce* (Free Press 2000)

Gregory, Raymond F., *Age Discrimination in the American Workplace*: Old at a Young Age (Rutgers, 2001)

Martin, Don, W, Martin, Betty, Woo, *Arizona in Your Future: The Complete Relocation Guide for Job-Seekers, Retirees and Snowbirds,* (Discover Guides 2002)

Pollan, Stephen, Levine, Mark, *"Second Acts" Creating the Life You Really Want, Building The Career You Truly Desire*, (Harper, 2002

Ray, Samuel, N, *Resumes for the Over-50 Job Hunger* (Wiley, 1993)

Rowe, John, Kahn, Robert, *Successful Aging*, (Dell 1999)

Schlossberg, Nancy, *Retire Smart Retire Happy: Finding Your True Path in Life* (APA 2004)

Sedlar, Jeri and Miners, Rick, *Don't Retire, Rewire!* (Alpha 2003)

Segrave, Kerry, Age *Discrimination by Employers* (McFarland, 2001)

Sheehy, Gail, Delbourgo, Joelle, *New Passages*, (Ballentine, 1996)

Sher, Barbara, *It's Only Too Late If You Don't Start Now* (Dell 1998)

Stone, Marika and Howard, Too Young to Retire: *101 Ways to Start the Rest of Your Life* (Plume 2004)

Strode, Molly, *Creating a "Spiritual Retirement"* (Skylight 2003)

Walker, Jean, Erickson, *The Age Advantage: Making the Most of Your Midlife Career Transition* (Penguin Putnam, 2000)

Weinstein, Bob, *"So What If I'm 50?": Straight Talk and Proven Strategies for Getting Hired in the Toughest Job Market Ever* (McGraw-Hill, 1995)

Zelinski, Ernie, *How to Retire Happy, Wild and Free* (Ten Speed Press 2004)

ARTICLES & SURVEYS

AARP Best Employers for Workers Over 50 Honorees for 2003
http://www.aarp.org/bestemployers/2003winners.html

Cornell Study of Retirement and Well-Being
http://www.blcc.cornell.edu/archives/misc/retirement_study.pdf;
http://www.news.cornell.edu/Chronicle/01/4.5.01/retire-couples.html

Dychtwald, Ken, "It's Time to Retire Retirement" *Harvard Business Review* March 2004
http://harvardbusinessonline.hbsp.harvard.edu/b02/en/common/item_detail.jhtml?id=R0403C

Great Jobs: Our Annual List
http://www.aarpmagazine.org/lifestyle/Articles/a2003-09-17-greatjobs.html

Lingren, Herbert L., "Communication: Key to Understanding in Marriage and Family Life" http://nuforfamilies.unl.edu/family/poscommmarriage.htm

"Make Age Irrelevant by Beating Negative Views," http://www.aarp.org/careers/Articles/a2002-12-10-makeageirrelevant.html

"Retirees Face Increased Premiums," by Janelle Carter, Associated Press 2002, http://www.firstcoastnews.com/health/articles/2002-12-06/health_insurance.asp)

Read, Katy, "When Just One of You is Retiring" *Reader's Digest* http://www.rd.com/common/nav/index.jhtml?articleId=9525334&channelId=2&subChannelId=11

"Staying Ahead of the Curve 2003: The AARP Working in Retirement Study" http://research.aarp.org/econ/multiwork.html

"The Five Roads to Self-Employment," by Drake Beam Morin: http://www.dbm.com/portal/public/dbmnav.nsf/b090a04a2fa1cdfc85256a5b00617a2a/35e69cb7f629f7bc88256a6f00741b91?OpenDocument&Highlight=0,retirement

WEB SITES

http://www.retirementwithapurpose.com
http://www.notyetretired.com
http://www.2young2retire.com
http://www.retirement360.com
http://www.retiredbrains.com/
http://www.seniors4hire.org/
http://www.seniorjobbank.com/
http://www.middleage.org
http://www.lifecoursenavigation.com
http://www.re-visioningretirement.com
http://www.dontretirerewire.com
www.focuscareer.com/retirement-career.cfm
www.go60.com
www.askelibrary.com
http://www.nwfusion.com/newsletters/careers/2002/01175561.html
http://www.globalassignment.com/10-22-99/retirement.htm
http://www.retirementliving.com/RLart105.htm

ABOUT THE AUTHOR

Marcia Bench is a world-renowned expert in the field of career and life coaching. A Master Certified Career Coach™ and nationally respected expert in the job/career transition field, she has been coaching and consulting both individual and corporate clients since 1986. She is CEO of Coaching and Training Solutions, and Founder/Director of Career Coach Institute, LLC.

A former attorney, Marcia has authored nearly 20 books, including *Career Coaching: An Insider's Guide* (Davies-Black) and corresponding workbooks and CD albums; *Thriving in Transition* (Simon & Schuster) and *When 9 to 5 Isn't Enough* (Hay House). Recently, she also completed two series of three books each: the Job/Career Design Series designed for individuals in transition, and the Practice-Building for Coaches Series for coaches desiring to launch and build their businesses.

Marcia has been a featured speaker/trainer at over 450 local, regional and national conferences, as well as a guest on numerous television and radio programs. Her mission is to help individuals and organizations chart their own unique course for success. Marcia has coached business owners as well as managers and executives from Fortune 500 firms, and has mentored dozens of coaches.

She was a Senior Vice President in a dot-com career management firm for nearly five years, and previously spent 10 years as President of New Work Directions, a business and consulting firm she founded. Ms. Bench developed her expertise in business start-up and management in part through her four years as a practicing attorney specializing in business and employment issues.

Marcia was founder and charter president of the Portland (Oregon) Metro Chapter of the Association of Career Professionals International. She is a current member of the International Coach Federation and the Association of Career Professionals International. Marcia's education includes a Juris Doctorate from Northwestern School of Law of Lewis & Clark College and a Bachelor of Science in Psychology from Western Oregon University. In addition, she is a Certified Career Management Practitioner through the International Board of Career Management Certification, a Certified Business Coach, a Certified Teleader and Master Certified Career Coach.

For further information or to contact Ms. Bench:
Coaching and Training Solutions
PO Box 5778
Lake Havasu City, AZ 86404
(928) 764-2870
ceo@coachingandtrainingsolutions.com
http://www.coachingandtrainingsolutions.com
http://www.careercoachinstitute.com

COACHING & TRAINING SOLUTIONS PRODUCT CATALOG

We hope that you are enjoying this Coaching and Training Solutions product! We have an ever-expanding catalog of content kits that can be completed by individuals as a self-paced learning program, used by trainers as content for training sessions, or blended with coaching to add value and structure to the coaching experience. If you would like more information about our kits, we encourage you to visit http://www.coachingandtrainingsolutions.com, or copy and complete this form and fax it to 866-226-2244. Our physical mailing address is CTS, PO Box 5778, Lake Havasu City, AZ 86404.

Name: _____

Address: _____

City, State, ZIP: _____

Country: _____

Home Telephone: _____

Work Telephone: _____

Fax: _____ Email: _____

How did you hear about us:

- ☐ Internet search
- ☐ Referred by a friend
- ☐ Heard one of the authors speak
- ☐ Read an article written by the authors
- ☐ Other: _____

Please send me information about:

- ☐ CTS Coach Training Programs
- ☐ CTS Career Development Programs
- ☐ CTS Management Development Programs
- ☐ CTS Retirement Planning Programs
- ☐ CTS Practice-Building Programs
- ☐ Speaking presentations
- ☐ Customized training for your organization
- ☐ Other: _____

Thank you for your request!